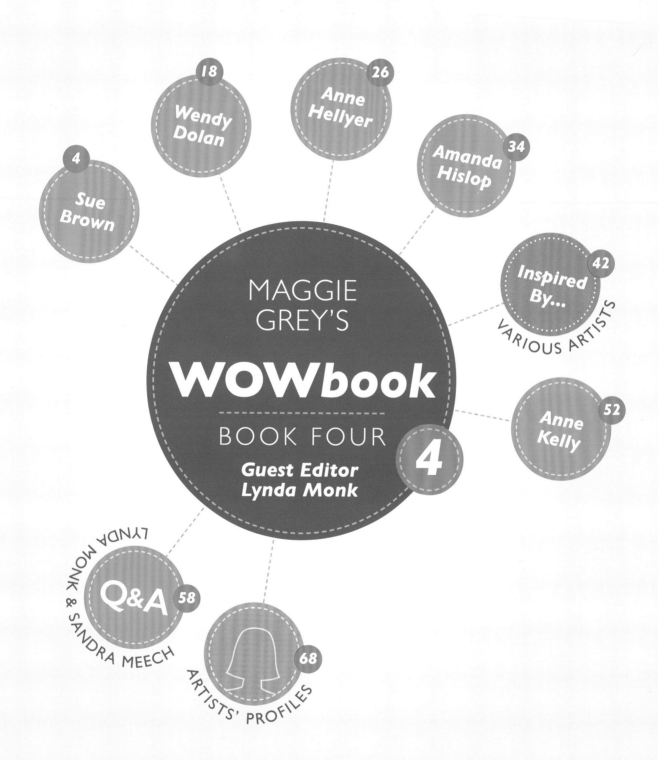

MAGGIE GREY'S

WOWbook

BOOK FOUR

4

Guest Editor
Lynda Monk

Welcome *to* WOWbook ④

BOOK FOUR

The team at **d4daisy** have been overwhelmed by the success of the WOWbook and having the linked website has extended the scope and made it so much more than just a book. To keep it fresh and exciting, we hit on the idea of having a guest editor for this issue – and who better than the versatile and creative Lynda Monk. We couldn't believe it when our first choice said 'yes'. But we're not losing Maggie, who is beavering away on the WOWbook website which promises to bring new delights with this book.

Over to Lynda ...

It has been an absolute joy working alongside Fiona as guest editor for this edition of the WOWbook. When Maggie asked if I would like to take this on, I thought it would be a breeze. I just didn't realise how hard the team and all the featured artists work to bring you such a superb publication.

We have some amazing artists in this issue sharing their techniques with you: Sue Brown uses transfer printing with gum arabic and a selection of images, Wendy Dolan shows us how to interpret a Gaudi design by layering fabrics and adding textural effects, Amanda Hislop uses a combination of acrylic paints and stitch to create an abstract landscape. With summer here, Anne Hellyer constructs a Cornish beach scene and last but not least, Anne Kelly transforms a pre-loved sewing box in memory of her grandmother.

For the celebrity interview, I had the pleasure of speaking to the very talented Sandra Meech, who shares with us her inspiration, favoured techniques and the thought processes behind her new work.

We have continued the 'Inspired by' theme with the letter B showcasing five different artists who have used themes beginning with this letter to create some very original work.

Being in the enviable position of reading through all the articles first, I just had to try out some of the techniques for myself – well, someone had to do it!

I have thoroughly enjoyed working through the articles and I do hope you will share your own creations with us in our private Facebook group.

Lynda Monk

∧ *Moths on Silk* by Sue Brown. These gum arabic prints on silk are from an installation inspired by the Museum in the Park, Stroud, Gloucestershire, UK's hidden moth collections. They were part of a wall of fluttering prints describing the delicate nature of cased moth collections from the 2018 exhibition 'Into the Light'.

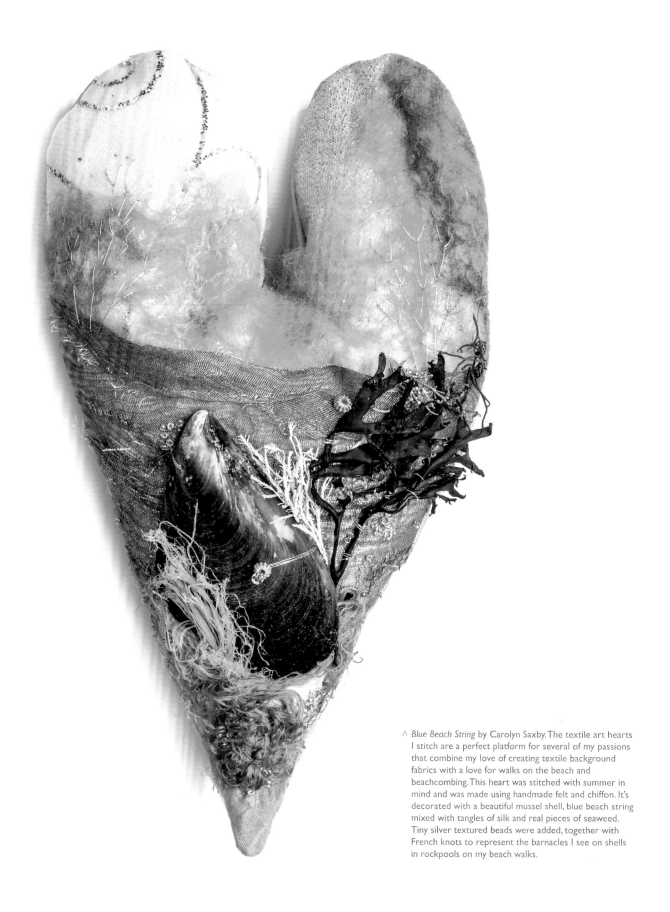

∧ *Blue Beach String* by Carolyn Saxby. The textile art hearts
I stitch are a perfect platform for several of my passions
that combine my love of creating textile background
fabrics with a love for walks on the beach and
beachcombing. This heart was stitched with summer in
mind and was made using handmade felt and chiffon. It's
decorated with a beautiful mussel shell, blue beach string
mixed with tangles of silk and real pieces of seaweed.
Tiny silver textured beads were added, together with
French knots to represent the barnacles I see on shells
in rockpools on my beach walks.

MAKING AN IMPRESSION
Gum arabic transfer printing

Sue Brown

In my opinion there is nothing more mouth-watering than a printed mark – but then I am, first and foremost, a printmaker.

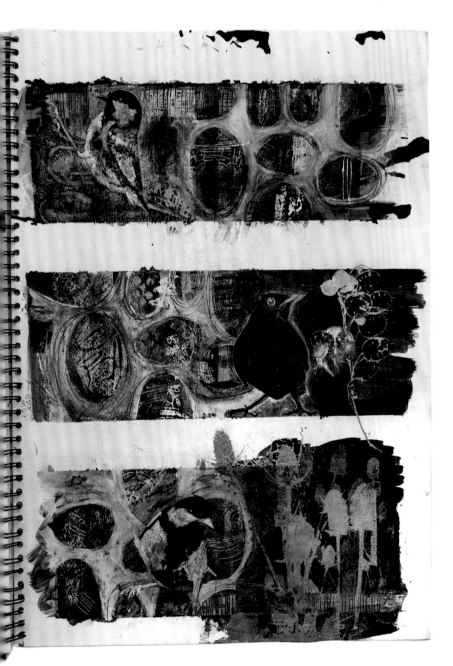

I have been making work by transferring ink from one surface to another for over twenty years. Mono printing, collagraph plates, dry points, lino and etchings are all surfaces that hold ink. Applying paper to that surface and either rubbing the back or pushing it through a press, the ink releases onto the surface creating surprise and planned marks. I have never painted directly onto a surface, although some say my sketchbooks have painting in them. Even in these pages there is print, that magical transfer from one surface to another, using paint, ink and gum arabic transfer printing.

What is gum arabic transfer printing?

Gum arabic transfer printing is sometimes known as paper lithography. For me, it has been a liberation; a technique that has allowed me to work through ideas in my sketchbooks and explore new substrates. I have been able to use my own images from photographs and drawings, allowing me to experiment with prints in my sketchbooks and developing rich, complex surfaces. The greatest revelation for me was applying the technique to fabric, pushing my practice in new directions.

< Sketchbooks using paint, ink and gum arabic transfer printing. Each sketchbook page starts off with a gum arabic transfer. Paint and Quink ink are layered over the images, bleached and printed over again. This creates layers of media over the page and gives the appearance of depth.

In simple terms, gum arabic transfer printing uses a photocopy as a printing plate. I first came across this technique when I was artist in residence for a local school. I was invited to accompany the sixth form on a field trip to Venice. I know, a tough job, but someone had to do it. It was my job to inspire the students with interesting techniques for their sketchbook practice. The only problem with this adventure was that Venice is all about buildings, which is the one thing I cannot draw. However, I had a couple of lucky finds just before I was due to go on this trip. One was a 1930s book with black and white photographs of Venice, and the other was a random Amazon purchase of the book *Collage Discovery* by Claudine Hellmuth. There was a short chapter describing the transfer technique using oil paints. As a printmaker with oil-based inks and gum arabic already in the studio, it was not such a giant leap to adapt the process, making it failsafe and easy to control. Together with the images photocopied from my 1930s resource, I was filling sketchbooks with prepared pages of Venetian scenes and then adding my own particular twist. The school is still using the process, ten years after my residency.

> Sketchbooks with mixed-media including gum arabic transfer printing using birds and insects for inspiration. I am often inspired by garden visitors and birds I see on walks, but I find entomological museum collections completely fascinating. I take many, many photographs to work from – the detail is very important.

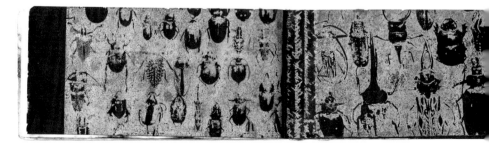

^ Sketchbooks from a
field trip to Venice using
the gum arabic transfer
printing method.
I prepared the pages with
Venetian scenes then
added my own twist. I like
the contrast of the man-
made background with a
natural motif.

Gum arabic transfer has become an important part of my sketchbook practice. It acts as a starting point for many of my drawings. I now use my own photographs of buildings and nature-inspired textural backgrounds, together with my drawings of birds and moths. I have started to make work using the technique as the main event and not just part of my pages. I recently showed a collection of prints on silk at the Museum in the Park, Stroud, Gloucestershire, UK.

∧ The installation of *Moths on Silk* was made purely of moth drawings and photographic backgrounds, transfer printed in layers and built-up coloured surfaces. The silk was soft enough to be displayed off the wall and fluttering. It is the fact that the technique retains the handle of the fabric printed on that I find interesting. It is also an excellent way of incorporating text into work, adding a photographic element to an image or creating backgrounds to work into.

MATERIALS

- Photocopied or laser printed images
- Substrate to print onto – cartridge paper, sketchbook or thin fabrics with no surface texture
- Gum arabic
- Linseed oil
- Oil-based printing ink (do not use Safe Wash inks)
- Non-stick baking paper (not greaseproof paper)
- Blotting paper
- 2 acetate sheets, plastic file covers or small sheets of perspex
- Brayer (roller)
- Garden spray bottle filled with water
- Cat litter tray or similar
- Wooden spoon

< A photographic image as a photocopy.

Gather your images together

Gum arabic transfer is one of the most flexible techniques I have ever used. You will need photocopies of the images you wish to transfer. The photocopies should be black and white with no greyscale. You can use copyright-free imagery, your own photographs or drawings but there are two things to consider. First, the image must have *no* greyscale – this can be achieved using an editing program on your computer or iPad. If you are using text, make sure you flip it so that it will print the right way around. The second thing – and this is really important: the copy must be printed with toner, either from a photocopier or a laser printer. Inkjet prints will not work. The print from toner is oil-based ink; the ink from an inkjet is water-based and will not accommodate the next process.

Before starting, have a pile of photocopies ready to use. Play around with scale, have larger and smaller versions of your image and also have several of the same size so that you can repeat your prints in different colours and compositions.

< Photocopies of my original drawings.

Getting started

You are now ready to print. Now is the time to choose your substrate. This could be sheets of cartridge paper, sketchbooks or fabrics, which will need to be ironed. Set aside some time to experiment – a couple of hours at least – as this makes it worthwhile getting ink out and clearing up at the end.

Before starting, gather together all the materials and equipment needed to make a transfer. Have everything to hand as the process moves along rapidly.

If your original copy is an inkjet print, mark it on the back and keep it completely separate from your photocopies. You can get more prints from this and there will be no mix-up with inkjet and toner prints.

Preparing the ink

1. Spread a small amount of ink onto your acetate sheet. I am using a cream coloured ink. The ink will need to be loosened with a small amount of linseed oil and mixed well. Too thick and the ink will not spray – too thin and the print will look light. The ink should drop slowly off a palette knife.

2. Ink up your roller ready to apply to the copy. The ink should be thin and the surface should resemble suede. Do not have the ink too 'juicy'.

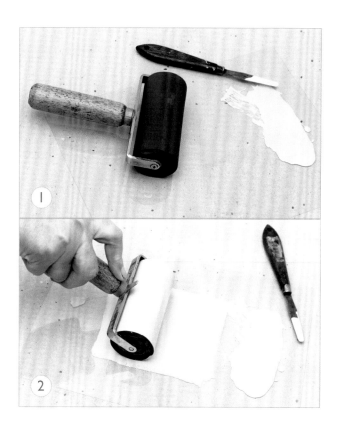

Applying the gum arabic

1. Lay your chosen photocopy face down onto a sheet of baking paper. Apply a small amount of gum arabic and smooth it across the back of the copy. Do not work the gum arabic into the paper – just smooth it over the surface, covering it completely.

2. Turn the copy over and repeat the process on the reverse. The copy should be quite wet.

3. Finally, pick up the copy and allow the excess fluid to drain off.

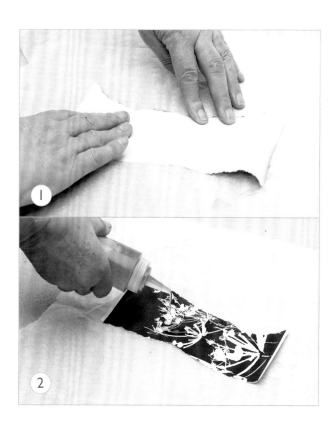

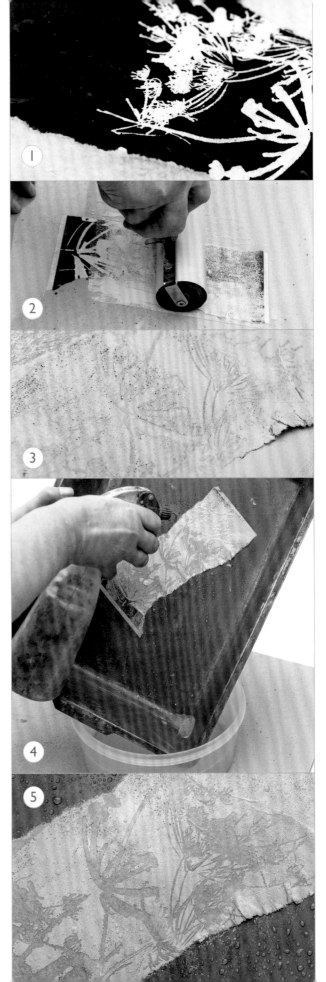

Inking

1. Lay the gummed copy, face up, onto the second piece of acetate to ink it. The gum arabic should be repelling the black photocopy ink.

2. Roll the loosened ink onto the copy with a brayer. Roll gently and repeatedly with thin layers of ink. Be careful that the copy doesn't roll itself around the brayer. Avoid this by rolling one way – from the middle to the outer edge.

3. Your copy should now be covered with thin layers of ink.

4. Place the copy into a plastic tray (such as a cat litter tray) and hold the tray upright over a sink or bucket. The tray prevents inky spray covering other surfaces. Spray the copy with water using a garden spray bottle.

5. As the copy is sprayed, the gum arabic dissolves from the white areas, taking the ink with it. This leaves the oil-based ink attached to the photocopy ink.

Stop spraying when you have achieved the look you require. You do not have to rinse all the ink off – you may want to leave some of the inked bits in places. Some inks take a while to remove but metallic inks tend to come off easily.

TIP
Try different inks and adjust the amount of linseed oil in the initial mix if you are not getting the desired effect.

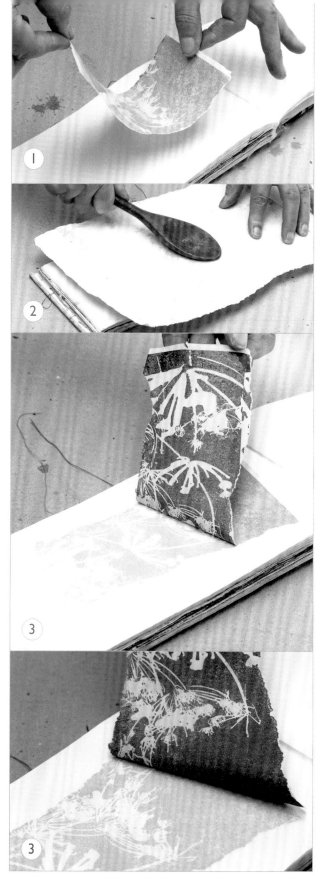

Printing

1. Take the inked and sprayed copy and lay it down, carefully, onto your chosen substrate. Place it inked side down. Avoid dragging, as the ink releases as soon as the copy touches the surface.

2. Cover the copy with blotting paper and gently rub with the back of a wooden spoon.

3. It's now time for the big reveal! Pull back the blotting paper and peel back the copy to reveal your print.

4. You can now overprint or work into this image without waiting for anything to dry. For those of us who just cannot wait, it is the ideal process for layering.

The beauty of this process is that you can print into a sketchbook or onto most paper surfaces with basic equipment. With the use of an etching press, you can take this technique to the next level.

Having experimented with gum arabic transfer over the years, I have discovered that there are very few surfaces you cannot print onto. In this article, I have referred to sketchbooks and paper although there is no reason why thin smooth fabrics cannot be used with the 'wooden spoon' method above.

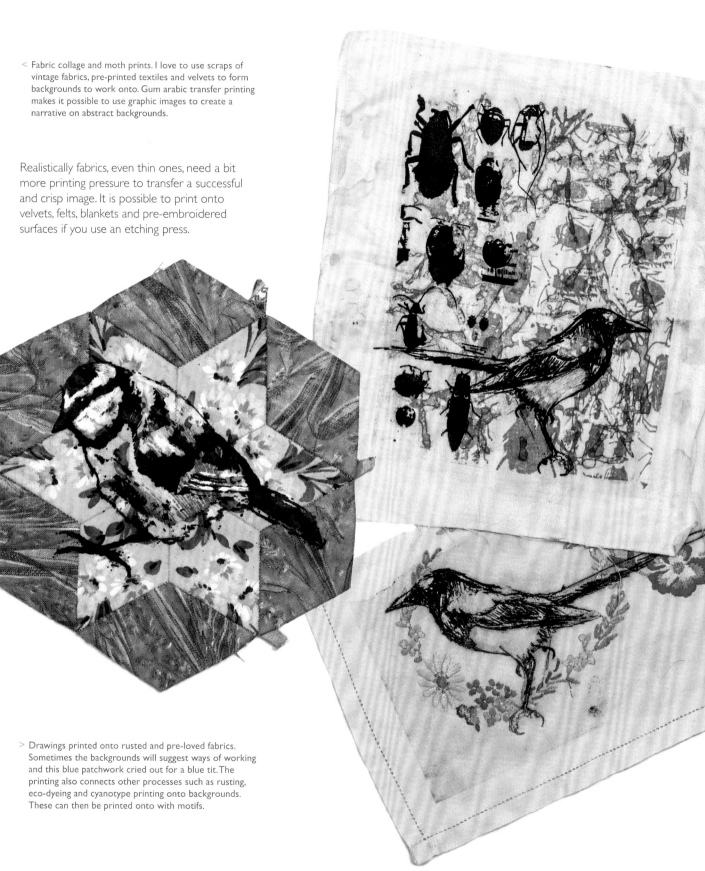

< Fabric collage and moth prints. I love to use scraps of vintage fabrics, pre-printed textiles and velvets to form backgrounds to work onto. Gum arabic transfer printing makes it possible to use graphic images to create a narrative on abstract backgrounds.

Realistically fabrics, even thin ones, need a bit more printing pressure to transfer a successful and crisp image. It is possible to print onto velvets, felts, blankets and pre-embroidered surfaces if you use an etching press.

> Drawings printed onto rusted and pre-loved fabrics. Sometimes the backgrounds will suggest ways of working and this blue patchwork cried out for a blue tit. The printing also connects other processes such as rusting, eco-dyeing and cyanotype printing onto backgrounds. These can then be printed onto with motifs.

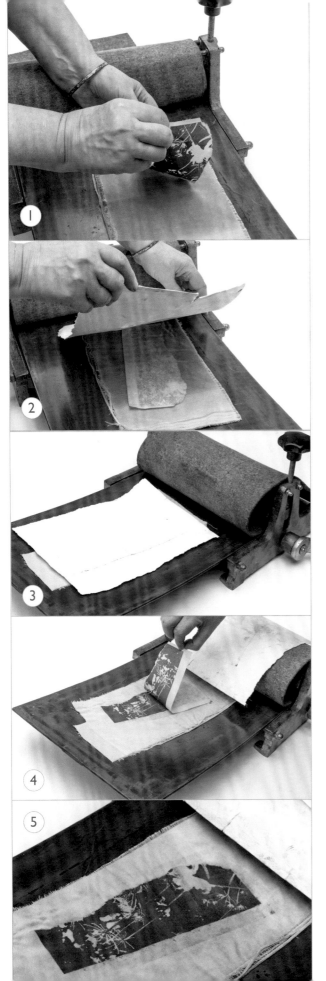

∧ An etching press.

Etching press method

To do this, follow the application instructions on pages 9 and 10 for the gum arabic and the inking method.

1. Lay your chosen fabric on the press bed. I have used velvet. Place your inked photocopy onto the fabric, face down.

2. Cover with blotting paper to absorb the excess moisture.

3. Pass everything through the press.

4. Remove the blotting paper and lift the photocopy.

5. Reveal the finished print. Again, you do not have to wait for this print to dry before overprinting with another image and colour.

I have been thrilled with the results of printing onto fabric and have successfully printed onto vintage embroidery, textile collages and velvets. Once the print is dry, there is a world of creative options open to you. Work further into the image using mixed-media, paint and ink.

Free machine or hand embroidery can be introduced as the fabric retains its handle. I have tried eco-printing onto transfer printed silk and have been surprised at how well the ink takes both boiling and washing.

∧ Eco-dyed and printed silk. It is surprising how well the gum arabic transfer prints cope with washing and, in this case, eco-dyeing. This is the limit of my dyeing experience; it will be interesting to see other techniques applied to this process.

< Cotton fabric book. An ideal use for textile samples is to make them into books. This is made from one piece of fabric and once folded, each page can be worked and developed individually.

∨ Mixed-media paper book. When teaching gum arabic transfer as a sketchbook workshop, I always encourage the making of paper samples into these simple, four-page booklets. It is completely satisfying to take several of these booklets home as a record of the processes learnt during a weekend.

It is exciting for me that this process can carry my rough designs through to a work in progress. It means that my sketchbook practice can be translated into finished pieces. I feel as though I have only scratched the surface of this technique and there are so many possibilities for it in textiles, artist book projects and other work.

∧ Cyanotype and linen fabric. I cannot resist continually experimenting with the printmaking technique and have many samples ready to incorporate into projects. Printing onto coloured linen and pre-cyanotype fabric feeds my curiosity. Cyanotype printing uses transparent, translucent or opaque objects to block light and make blue images on cloth or paper. Pre-treated sheets of fabric can be purchased which make the process safer and easier.

> Collagraph bird print with transfer printed background and stitch. I am now developing projects incorporating my first love, collagraph printmaking with gum arabic transferred images. I love the way the silk takes the printed image so crisply. It is not a huge leap from printing onto paper, as paper is just another fibre. I am looking forward to developing more works on silk and embellishing the pieces with stitched elements. Collagraph prints are made by preparing a textured plate which is sealed and inked before being put through a press.

GUIDED BY GAUDI
Layered, painted and stitched

Wendy Dolan

Architecture can provide us with a wide source of inspiration for textile design work. Doors, windows, arches and balustrades provide ideal starting points and different textures can create exciting surfaces – rough brickwork, peeling plaster, smooth stonework and roof tiles.

The Spanish architect Antoni Gaudi designed some amazing buildings based on organic shapes and symbolism, many of which can be seen in Barcelona. One of his most fascinating and intriguing masterpieces is the church crypt at Colonia Güell, a purpose-built industrial village south-west of Barcelona, now declared a UNESCO World Heritage Site. The entire building combines interesting shapes and textures and I am particularly drawn to the stained glass windows and the surrounding roof tiles. Viewed closely, you can see the shapes of the glass window panes, protected by a grating which was made from discarded weavers' needles from the Güell Colony factory. The recesses around the windows are decorated with mosaic tiles and the roof tiles themselves are rough and uneven. I chose these different elements to create the design shown in this workshop.

> Pages from my sketchbook showing my drawings of the church crypt at Colonia Güell, Barcelona, Spain, designed by Antoni Gaudi. I drew the stained glass windows with surrounding mosaics and the textured brickwork, which I then coloured.

I love working with texture and I hope this workshop will encourage you to create interesting surfaces by layering fabrics, adding textural effects and applying freehand stitching.

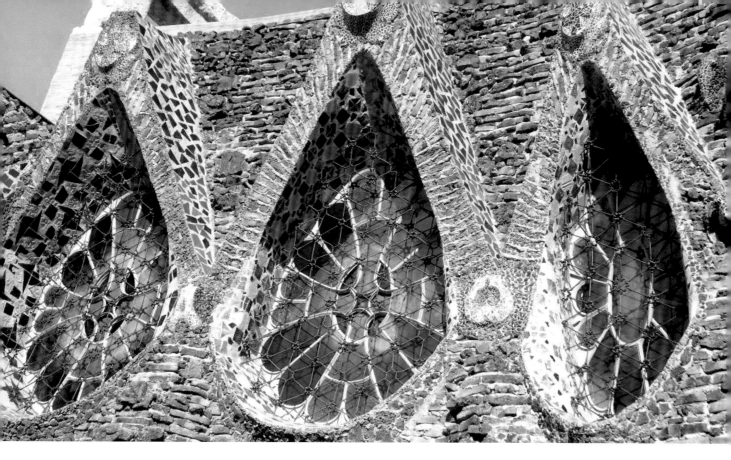

MATERIALS AND EQUIPMENT

- Sewing machine with freehand embroidery/ darning foot
- Embroidery scissors
- Pins
- Iron and ironing surface
- Heat gun
- Baking parchment
- Fabric paints
- Xpandaprint
- Brushes, sponges and palette knife
- Wooden skewer
- Paper doily
- Coloured papers
- Tracing paper, pencil and marker pen
- Glue stick
- Masking tape
- Pre-washed calico
- Selection of natural, pre-washed textured fabrics (I have used silk noil and cotton scrim)
- Tear away stabiliser (I used Stitch n Tear)
- Coloured sheer fabrics such as organza or chiffon
- White or cream cotton machine thread
- Coloured machine embroidery threads
- Coloured threads for hand stitching (optional)

Design

Select several images from your chosen design source and draw or trace them individually. If you are using images from the internet, don't forget to check for copyright first. You can then move them around, planning your composition and perhaps varying the scale as you work. When you are happy with your design, trace it onto a sheet of tracing paper using a fine black marker pen. Mark the top edge so you know which is the right side.

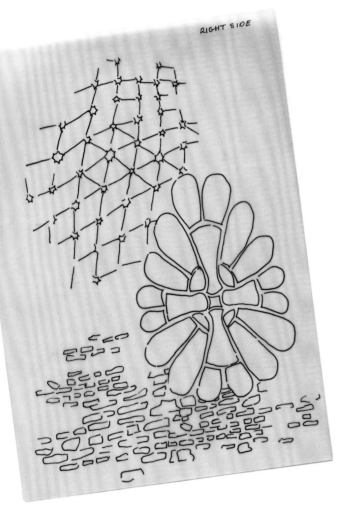

Colour – paper collage

Consider using a limited colour scheme. Select a range of papers varying in tone from light to dark. Tear into strips and arrange on a backing paper with your tracing hinged with masking tape on top. You will be able to keep raising the tracing as you position torn strips of paper in a balanced arrangement underneath. My paper strips are positioned to reflect the vertical and horizontal elements of the design. Vary the width and length of the papers as you tear. Secure with a glue stick.

Preparing your fabric background

1. Take a piece of calico, slightly larger than your image size, and place it on a larger piece of backing calico.

2. Position your tracing, right side up, onto the centre and attach along the top edge with hinges of masking tape. You will now be able to raise and lower the tracing as you position torn strips of fabric in a balanced arrangement underneath.

3. Select fabrics with varying textures and tear them to add to the surface interest. I have used calico and silk noil. Vary the textures, widths and lengths of the fabric strips and position according to the vertical or horizontal nature of your design.

4. Pin in place.

5. Attach a piece of Stitch n Tear stabiliser behind the work with a couple of pins.

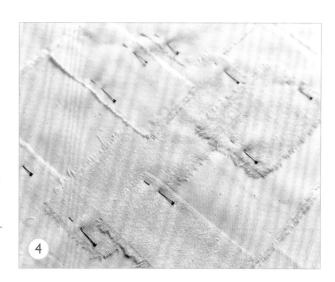

Stitching the background

1. Set up your machine for freehand machine embroidery. Remove the presser foot and replace with a freehand embroidery or darning foot. Lower or cover the teeth or feed dogs and set your stitch length to 0. You will now be in control of the stitch length and direction. Don't forget to lower the presser foot lever, engaging the top thread tension, and bring the bobbin thread to the surface.

2. Using white or cream cotton thread, stitch down the fabric strips.

3. You can now add additional texture with loosely woven scrim in the areas where there may be rough texture or weathering. I have concentrated on the roof tiles.

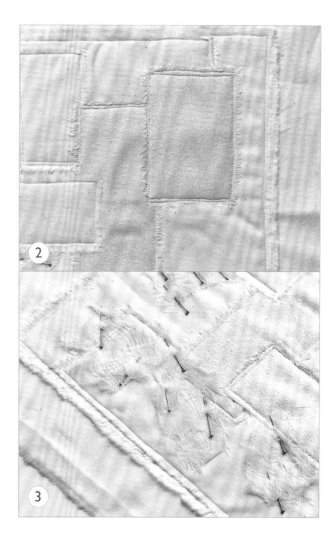

TIP
A wooden skewer can help hold the fabrics in place as you remove the pins to stitch.

Xpandaprint

This three-dimensional medium is ideal for creating crumbly textures.

1. Use a dry sponge and gently apply to the required areas.

2. Working on a heatproof surface, use a hot air tool to heat the paste, holding the tool approximately 4 in (10 cm) away from the fabric. Alternatively, you can cover the surface with non-stick baking paper and hover a hot iron over the surface. Be patient as it may take a while for the crusty results to appear. You will see interesting effects where the scrim shows through. Handle the hot air tool and the iron with care, in a well ventilated area.

Adding colour

Your textured background is now ready to paint. Mix your paints according to your chosen colour scheme. I used water-based, iron-fixed fabric paint. Try not to make the colours too dark and always test first. Lightly spray the surface with water before painting to allow the colours to blend. Using your paper collage as a reference, paint in the areas of colour with a brush. Iron to fix, taking care not to flatten the Xpandaprint textures.

TIP
When fixing the paint, use baking paper to protect the Xpandaprint texture while ironing, or use a hairdryer.

< Use fabric paint to colour your textured background.

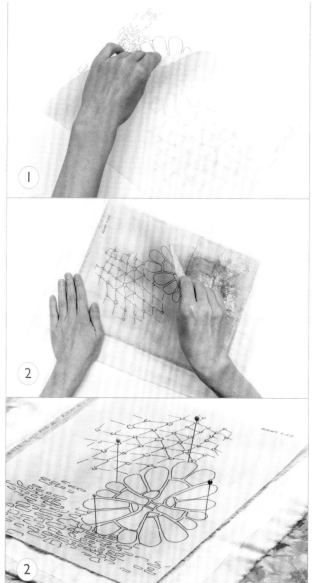

Transferring the design

You can transfer the design by stitching from the reverse.

1. Take your tracing and lay it upside down on the table. Place a piece of Stitch n Tear stabiliser on top and copy the image using a hard pencil (this is now a reverse image). Keep to one side.

2. To register the design in position, place the tracing right side up on your painted fabric and mark three or four dominant points with pins, pushing them through to the back.

3. Turn the fabric over and mark these pin points with a pencil on the reverse.

4. Take your Stitch n Tear copy of the image and line up the pencil marks with the relevant points. Pin in place.

5. You can now start to stitch the design from the back, transferring the image as you stitch. Thread your machine with a dark colour in the bobbin and on top. Tighten your top tension slightly to prevent bobbling.

6. The bobbin thread creates the outline on the right side of the fabric. Check your thread tensions as you stitch.

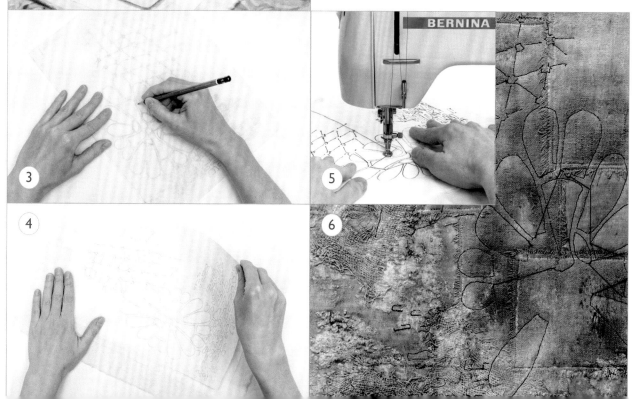

Surface embellishment

1. Having transferred the design you are now ready to work on the right side. Sheer fabrics can be applied to create a stained glass effect.

2. Overlay the fabric, stitch around the shapes, then cut away the excess. I have used this technique on the grating as well.

3. Now enjoy stitching into your work. You are adding to the surface texture as well as emphasising the design.

4. Several rows of straight stitch and narrow satin stitch can accentuate lines. Dense areas of stitching, for example granite stitch and random 'shaky' zigzag, can create raised texture. Try to use a variety of threads and remember to keep standing back from your work to consider the balance. Hand stitching can be added at any stage – and remember: you are making marks with thread.

Mosaic effects

Mosaic patterns adorn many of Gaudi's structures including the surrounds of the chapel windows. To add a mosaic effect, I have stencilled paint through a paper doily.

∨ To add a mosaic effect, stencil paint through a paper doily.

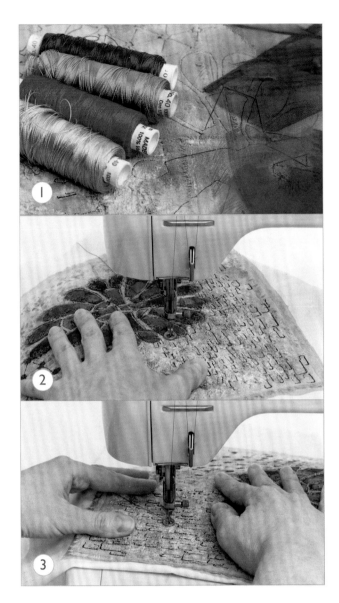

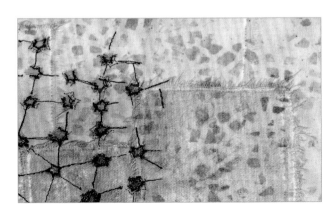

Finished piece

Here is my finished piece: my Gaudi inspired panel. I hope you enjoy experimenting with the techniques in this workshop and exploring the wonderful shapes and designs in Gaudi's architecture.

∧ Finished piece. A Gaudi inspired panel using layered fabrics and paint, embellished with freehand machine and hand stitching.

DOUBLE VISION
Appliqué and machine embroidered seaside village

∨ *Chi an mor*. House by the sea. My completed piece made with hand painted fabric backed with fusible webbing. This has then been appliquéd to a backing and enhanced with paint and free machine embroidery.

Anne Hellyer

I have named this piece *Chi an mor* which is an old Cornish phrase meaning 'house by the sea'. It was inspired by a visit to Cornwall, UK, where I stood high on Bodmin Moor and could see the sea on both sides of the land; a double-sided view. This piece reflects this two-sided view with one side reflecting the sea and the other, the countryside. It was made using my hand painted fabric with appliqué and free machine embroidery.

TIP
To tie the design together, use the same threads for two different areas, for example, the sea and the blue paintwork, and the ploughed field and the wall.

MATERIALS

- Medium-weight calico, hand painted in different colours
- Fusible webbing
- S80 Vilene
- Small pieces of scrim (optional)

YOU WILL ALSO NEED:

- Sewing machine with darning/embroidery foot
- A size 14/90 standard or topstitch needle
- Machine threads to match your fabric colours
- Acrylic paints in your chosen colours (white, yellow, green, blue, etc.)
- Sharpie pens or similar

Some tips before you start

Please read through *ALL* the instructions before you begin this workshop.

- Refer to the main pictures throughout to give you inspiration and ideas.
- Overlap the fabrics where possible so that you only have one raw edge to neaten, for example, the roof over the top of the houses and one field over the edge of another, etc.
- Anchor the beginning and end of each section of machined zigzag stitch with a couple of straight stitches.
- Neaten raw edges with zigzag stitch and add other details with both zigzag and straight stitches.

Preparing your fabric

I like to hand paint my calico but you could use plain coloured, medium-weight fabrics from your stash, should you wish.

This is how I paint my fabrics:

1. I prefer to use a student quality paint such as Dale Rowney or Winsor & Newton acrylics. However, if you have the ready diluted acrylic paints then play with those first as you can still achieve some interesting results.

2. Dilute the acrylic paint with water in your chosen colours to the consistency of milk. Wash out any dressing from the medium-weight calico and while the fabric is still wet, paint it with the diluted solution of paint. Cover the whole of the piece of fabric with a base colour and then add accent colours if you wish.

3. Screw up the wet painted fabric into a ball and place on a polythene sheet. Leave to dry. *Do not leave it to dry on paper as it will stick!*

4. It will take a minimum of two to three days to dry, depending on the weather and the size of your piece of fabric. When the fabric is dry, it may feel hard but once you flatten and iron it, the plastic content of the acrylic paint softens and the fabric becomes very pliable. It is the plastic content in acrylic paint that makes it safe to stitch with a sewing machine as the paint will not powder and clog your machine's working parts.

5. Make sure you cover the surface of the painted fabric with baking paper before ironing to protect your iron and fabric. Iron fusible webbing onto the back of all your fabric pieces once they are dry. Keep the backing paper attached until you are ready to fuse the fabric to your S80 Vilene.

TIP
Screwing the fabric into a ball means that the pigment in the paint runs into the creases and folds. You could try experimenting with folding your painted fabric instead.

Preparing the Vilene and fabric

1. Cut two pieces of S80 Vilene to shape, following the measurements in diagram 1. One piece will be the front view and the other, the back.

2. Cut one piece of S80 Vilene for the boat in diagram 2.

3. Cut the building and roof shapes in fabric backed with fusible webbing as shown in diagram 2.

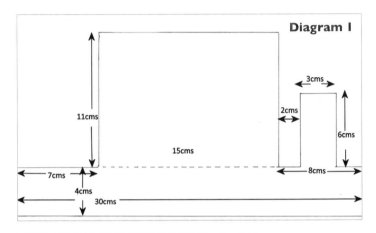

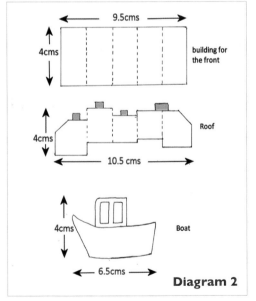

∧ Diagram 1.
The dimensions and outline for the S80 Vilene backing.

< Diagram 2.
The dimensions for details within both the front and back views.

> The field and small houses have been bonded into position. The bottom of both will be covered once the sea wall is bonded into place.

Getting started

The front view

1. Cut a piece of green hand painted fused calico 6 x 4½ in (15 x 12 cm). This will represent the field. Bond this to the front of the S80 Vilene shape, making sure you overlap onto the 'wall' – the long shape that runs along the bottom edge.

2. Place the building in position on top of the field. Use small pieces of fabric to represent chimneys and place them on the background. Now add the roof, making sure to overlap the top of the buildings and the bottoms of the chimneys. Iron all pieces thoroughly to bond them in place.

3. Draw in the windows with a black Sharpie pen and add your doors with a coloured Sharpie pen. *NOTE:* Be careful as Sharpie pens bleed slightly. This edge will be covered with stitch so no need to worry too much.

4. Stitch your gutters and drainpipes with a zigzag stitch. The gutters neaten the lower raw edge of the roof. Neaten the rest of the roof and chimneys with further zigzag stitch. Next, add window and door frames with a straight stitch. Stitch in as little or as much detail as you like.

5. Shape and trim the background into a 'hill', keeping it as large as possible.

> The completed houses. I have added doors and windows with Sharpie pens and have then used free machine embroidery to add further details, a hint of roof tiles, window frames, etc. All raw edges have been neatened with free machine zigzag stitch, except for the lower edge as this will be covered by the sea wall. The door knobs were hand stitched with French knots.

< Once the front has been
  shaped, it can be used
  as a template for the
  rear view. Cut the back
  slightly larger, as shown
  here. It makes it easier
  to stitch the two pieces
  together accurately at
  the end.

The rear view

1. Use the front view as a template by laying
   it on top of the second piece of your S80
   Vilene and drawing around the shape. Cut just
   slightly outside of your drawn lines to make
   this piece fractionally larger.

2. Create a patchwork of fields in hand painted
   green and brown calico and fuse these in
   place, ensuring that the bottom field overlaps
   the wall.

3. Add a small house using the same method
   and pieces of the same fabrics you used
   on the front section. It can be positioned
   anywhere on the hill, or even tucked behind
   the hill to give a sense of depth. Add the
   chimney and roof, and draw in the windows.
   Stitch in the same way as you did the row of
   cottages on the front. This adds continuity to
   your piece and ties the design together.

4. Add further details to the fields, fences,
   hedges and trees with stitch and small pieces
   of painted scrim.

5. To stitch the tree trunk, place two or three
   layers of painted or coloured scrim above the
   trunk and use straight stitch to signify branches.
   Cut back or trim the scrim into shape, adding
   more if required.

6. I like to hand stitch sheep using cotton perle
   French knots and black stranded cotton onto
   my hand painted calico.

TIP
Paint small
pieces of scrim
in different colours,
using the same
method as you did
for painting your
calico.

< I have used both hand
  and machine stitch to
  add texture and depth,
  with a variegated thread
  for the ploughed field.

< Free machine
  embroidery has been
  used to create the
  trees and hedges with
  small pieces of hand
  painted scrim added for
  extra texture.

< For my sheep I drew the
  outline of the body onto
  the fabric before starting,
  filling in the outline with
  the French knots. Two
  strands of black stranded
  cotton were used to
  add the head and legs.
  My sheep look to the
  side or facing the front,
  for a more quizzical look.

∨ Fusible webbing is bonded to fabric
and the waves are drawn on the
backing paper before cutting out.

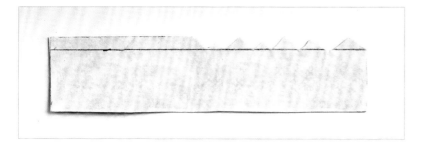

∨ Front view with all stitching
completed. I checked my design
to ensure I had added enough
stitch details to the buildings,
wall, lighthouse and sea.

The wall, the lighthouse and the sea

1. The next step is to stitch the wall on both the front and back pieces. You will need two pieces of fabric, one for each side measuring 12 x 1 in (30 x 2.5 cm). Bond the fabric directly to the S80 Vilene shape. Add stone-shaped stitching or just a hint of a structure. Neaten the top of the wall with zigzag stitch, only where it adjoins the buildings on the front and the fields at the back.

2. For the lighthouse, bond a piece of calico 2½ x 1 in (6 x 2.5 cm) in place on both the front and the back of your work. Use yellow and white acrylic paint, Sharpie pens and stitch to add more detail.

3. Cut two pieces of sea-coloured calico 12 x 1 in (30 x 2.5 cm). Cut a wave design into each and bond one piece on each of the walls on the front and back. Stitch the waves to anchor it in place. The S80 Vilene should now be completely covered.

Check that you are happy with your finished front and back views. Now you are ready to stitch them together. I find it makes it easier if you hold the two pieces together with quilting or bulldog clips, if you have them. Straight stitch around the whole of the outer edge – as near to the edge as you can. Once the two sides are firmly attached, trim off any excess fabrics and use a zigzag stitch to neaten around the whole of the outside. You can do this in one colour or change colours to match the fabrics as you go.

< Completed back view. With this art piece, the back view is as important as the front so I spend time checking my design to ensure I am happy with the stitched details added and that my overall design is balanced. As well as the building, wall, lighthouse and sea on this side, there are the fields and sheep.

TIP
To ensure the sea doesn't go uphill, measure half a centimetre from the top of each piece and draw a line across. The trough of each wave should be cut to this line.

< The completed boat and waves. The strips of sea to make the bay, including the boat, are completely stitched before being applied to the main structure.

The boat

1. Fuse fabric to both sides of the boat shape. The height of the hull in my design is oversized so that it can easily be positioned to sit on the waves.

2. If you wish, you could paint above the hull with white paint. Add windows to the front with the black Sharpie pen.

3. Neaten all but the bottom edge with a zigzag stitch.

The sea

1. Cut one piece of S80 Vilene measuring 11½ × 1 in (29 × 2.5 cm) and one piece 7½ × 1 in (19 × 2.5 cm). These are for the strips of sea across the bay.

2. Take your first piece of S80 Vilene – the one measuring 11½ × 1 in (29 × 2.5 cm) – and bond the sea fabric to the right side. Draw the waves on the back. Important: to ensure the sea doesn't go uphill, measure half a centimetre from the top of each piece and draw a line across. The trough of each wave should be cut to this line.

3. Cut off the excess fabric and interfacing. Stitch the wave pattern. Now cut this strip into two pieces, one measuring 5 in (13 cm) and the other 6 in (16 cm).

4. Place the boat somewhere along the 6 in (16 cm) piece and stitch into place.

5. Now, bond fabric to the back of these two pieces, cut away the excess fabric from the waves and anchor with straight stitch around all the edges. You will find that it is better to do the majority of stitch before adding these final layers of fabric as there is less bulk.

6. Take the strip of S80 Vilene measuring 7½ × 1 in (19 × 2.5 cm) and a piece of sea fabric the same size. Bond the fabric to the front side. Cut waves into the top and stitch the wave patterns.

7. Bond another piece of fabric to the back of this strip and cut away the excess from the waves. Anchor with straight stitch as before.

Finishing

1. You are now ready to attach the sea strips to finish construction. Starting with the 5 in (13 cm) strip, measure 2½ in (6.5 cm) in from the left edge of the front and attach in place with zigzag stitch.

2. Bend the wall and attach the other end of the strip 2¾ in (7 cm) in from the right edge.

3. Repeat with the 6 in (16 cm) strip with the boat. This time, the piece should be attached 1½ in (4 cm) from either end.

4. The final strip measuring 7½ × 1 in (19 × 2.5 cm) should be attached about ¾ in (1.5 cm) from either end.

I do hope you enjoy constructing your own *Chi an mor*. Don't forget to read through all the instructions before beginning this workshop. I can't wait to see your own versions of my house by the sea.

> My finished piece *Chi an mor* (House by the sea). The top photo shows the front view with the row of houses, the sea and the little boat. The bottom one is the other view with fields, a cottage and some grazing sheep.

UNFOLDING STORY
Winter tree lines – an abstract landscape

30 Jan 2019

∧ A collection of small A6 stitch-bound sketchbooks in landscape format, allowing an extended landscape across the page.

< An extended fragment drawing in Inktense pencils.

Amanda Hislop

The landscape around me, close to home, is an essential source of inspiration with particular elements that catch my eye again and again in my work: trees, hedges, the curve in a road. I find I am drawn to land lines and edges, seeking out the places where change happens in the landscape. My many sketchbooks recording personal observations and responses are well-thumbed companions and an inspiring resource to dip in and out of as the mood takes me. My preference is for my work to grow and evolve with no two pieces the same, but with a commonality in that they are linked by personal observations, drawings and memories of a place.

^ My scribble sketch drawing in
fine black pen of local trees.

My sketchbooks are a place to be free and to explore, with observation, imagination and inspiration playing equal parts. Working with thoughtful observation of lines within landscape, taking the land back to its bare form, simplifying; a way of looking, distils thoughts and records the essence of the place. In the 1980s, I studied woven textiles with painting at West Surrey College of Art and Design in Farnham, Surrey, UK. One of the most valuable skills this training taught me was to look closely and record in detail responses to textures, line, colour and form, now long practised and an ingrained habit which is part of me.

Moving in the landscape either walking or driving gives an ever changing view, with elements within appearing to move, offering a constantly changing perspective. Travelling through the landscape, I observe this moving panorama, fleeting glimpses of which are recorded in memory and then on paper to flow from my hand when sitting down and thinking 'landscape'.

∨ Winter trees landscape in a folded form. An informal folded concertina book on khadi cotton rag paper with brown paper collage elements, reflecting on trees in the landscape. A combination of observation, inspiration and imagination worked in pen with subtle washes of Inktense colour.

< A hard-backed concertina book compiled of elements of trees within the landscape. A combination of mono printed, drawn and collaged fragments, worked with ink pens and Inktense colour washes and highlights.

∨ A flat view of the concertina book showing some details of the drawings and collaged elements contained within the pages. Worked in pen and wash with wax resist, collage and coloured highlights in Inktense colour.

In my current work, folded forms and scrolls have become a means to reflect on landscape without the constraint of a traditional 'frame' format. With the folded or scroll form, I am able to explore the nature of the landscape as it unfolds around me, capturing surprise elements and playing with the idea of reveal and conceal within the folds or roll of the form.

∨ A rolled landscape form with part of the 'view' revealed, showing elements of painted layers and stitched drawing. Worked on layered papers on muslin cloth with painted layers of acrylic colour and elements of stitched drawing.

< Detail of my rolled landscape form, stitched and painted trees.

∨ A small rolled form; a monotype print with layers of acrylic colour on teabag paper bonded to openweave cotton scrim. This was worked with simple hand stitch in coloured threads and supported on fragments of found wood.

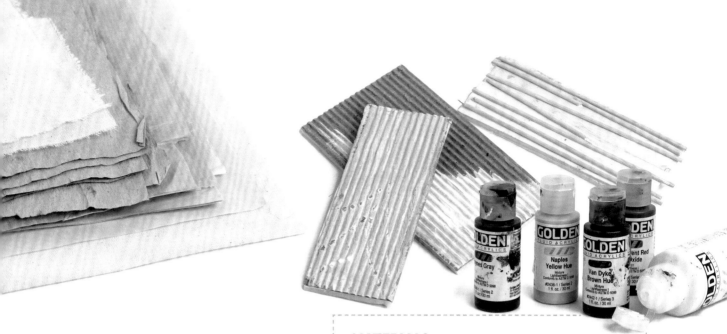

This workshop explores some of these ideas, giving an insight into the way I combine my love of drawing, painting and stitch.

In this workshop, the linear qualities of winter trees are captured using a combination of printed line and texture with elements of drawn lines worked in Inktense pencil. These lines are further developed with layers of stitch 'drawing'. The image expands across a narrow height and wide length format to create an extended landscape in collage worked with drawn stitched lines.

Please read through ALL the instructions before you start.

∨ Finished papers.

MATERIALS

- A piece of calico approximately 5½ × 37½ in (14 × 95 cm) and a selection of small pieces for printing
- Small pieces of teabag paper, lens tissue and found papers
- A small jar of CMC thickener cellulose paste (mixed with 1 tablespoon PVA glue) and a paste brush
- Acrylic paint in a limited palette (I have used Payne's grey, Naples yellow, transparent red iron oxide, Van Dyke brown hue, and white)
- Paint palette
- Paint brushes (wide flat or number 12 round)
- Thin clear plastic, slightly larger than the calico cloth
- Piece of candle wax
- Inktense pencils in grey or sepia
- Spray bottle with water
- Acrylic wax (for finishing the piece)
- Print blocks made from kebab sticks and corrugated card (use contact adhesive to secure the kebab sticks to the card)
- Sewing machine with feed dogs and embroidery foot, with threads in grey, dark and mid tones

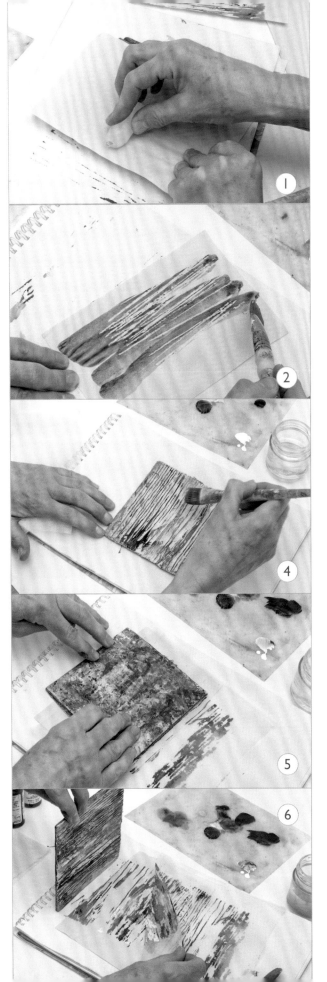

Printing

Begin by preparing a selection of small pieces of paper using candle-wax rubbings and a painterly approach to print.

1. Take a piece of paper. I have used newsprint. Lay it on the surface of a print block and, with the candle wax, use firm pressure to take a rubbing of the surface. The paper can be moved to create additional lines, if desired. You could also use coloured wax crayons in any combination of colours to suit your individual approach.

2. Mix a little water with your chosen acrylic colour to create a wash. Apply this to the surface of the rubbing, revealing a negative image of the print block. Make a series of these on different papers to use in the collage process. Here you can experiment with coloured wax and coloured washes, creating a whole series of papers to be used in future projects.

3. Prepare a firm flat surface for printing, such as a piece of card or an old newspaper. Use a sheet of paper as a backing to catch any overprinted lines. This can also be a source of lines to use in your work. Have your selection of papers to hand, ready for printing. Lay your first sheet on the print surface.

4. Choose your selected colour palette. I have used fluid acrylic colour in Payne's grey, Naples yellow, Van Dyke brown, transparent red iron oxide, and white. Use a brush to mix the undiluted acrylic colour and apply to the print block. Paint the colour across the surface, dipping your brush in water as you are working. This creates subtle blending and mingling of colour producing a 'painterly' effect. If you are using thicker acrylic paint, you will need to add a little more water to loosen the consistency of the paint. Allow yourself some experimentation with colour mixing if you are not familiar with this. Work on paper, making a note of the colours you have used and the mixes achieved.

5. Turn the block over and place, paint side down, on the paper. Apply firm pressure with the heel or edge of your hand to transfer the print onto the paper surface.

6. Carefully lift up the block along one edge to reveal the print. If your print is too faint, lay it back down and apply further pressure with your hand. In this example, I have layered lens tissue over newsprint paper to give a double print. Depending on the amount of paint you have used, you can sometimes make a secondary print which will be less distinct; experiment with the process.

∧ A small batch of papers ready for working into the folded form.

Preparing to stitch

Continue with the process until you have a small batch of papers ready for working into the folded form. You can vary the colour and application of the paint; adding water to the colour will create a more fluid print with colours blending in subtle ways. Overprinting is also an option to give layers and depth. Make some prints on small pieces of calico and try layering the teabag paper and lens tissue to create a double print. The aim is to create a batch of varied linear marks which can be used to suggest the lines of trees in the landscape.

1. Lay out your prints on your work surface. Spend some time selecting those you wish to use. You should have more than enough for this project and some may spark an idea for future exploration! Fragment the pieces using a combination of cutting and tearing, so that you have contrasting edges. Mix the lines, colours and textures from different prints. Take your piece of plastic and place this under the calico strip. Lay out your pieces of printed papers and cloth, moving them around, leaving gaps and rearranging until you are happy with the layout. You could take a photograph to record layout variations and then choose your favourite. Pin in place.

2. Using the cellulose and PVA glue mix, paste the pieces in place using a bristle brush. Lift the papers, section by section, and apply the paste to the calico, working to the edges of the cloth. Lay the paper section down and use the brush to work the printed paper or cloth into the surface. Continue until all sections are pasted on the cloth. Use your hands to smooth the surface and squeeze out any excess paste. Leave to dry on a flat surface.

3. At this stage, I use Inktense pencils to draw lines to suggest trees across the width of the piece, working with the printed background, adding another layer to the printed marks. You may choose to do this in specific areas across the piece, depending on the effect you wish to achieve. I like to have variety in a composition, echoing what I have seen in the natural landscape.

4. When you are happy with these tree lines, use a water spray to fix the Inktense pigment to the piece. This fixes the drawn line without disturbing the Inktense pigment. Use a brush to apply water if you prefer. Leave to dry on a flat surface or speed up the drying time with a hairdryer.

Stitching

The piece is now ready to stitch. I have worked with a dark grey thread through the needle and a mid tone in the bobbin. Set up your sewing machine with the feed dogs down, fit an embroidery foot and select straight stitch with the stitch length on 0. You will control the stitch length with the movement of the piece under the needle. Keep the machine at a constant, comfortable speed.

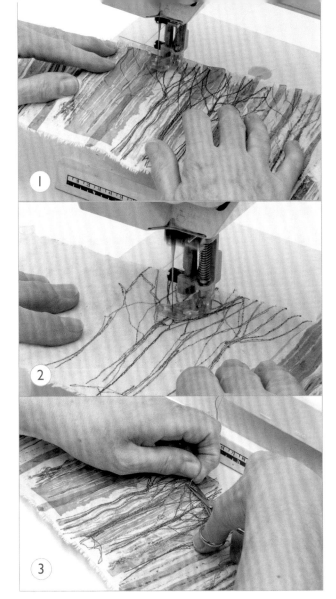

1. Working with the Inktense lines as a guide, draw with stitch to create layers of lines to represent trees. Keep the lines simple and expressive, varying the stitch length by the speed at which you move the fabric. A fast machine speed and slow movement gives a pleasing, fine expressive line.

2. Now that you have some stitch established on the front of the piece, turn it over and work from the reverse to add further expressive lines. The bobbin thread will show on the front giving a contrast. Working from the reverse allows freedom in stitch. This technique encourages a free approach as your mind is not distracted by following the image established on the front surface. Further lines can be worked from the front, if you wish. You can repeat this process to create denser stitching in some areas. I prefer not to waste time unpicking a line that seems out of place; I just work over it with another line and make it work with the stitching.

3. When you are satisfied with the stitch, tidy up any thread ends with a pair of sharp scissors. As an alternative, these ends could become a feature in the piece, with further stitch added together with hand stitch.

Folding

Now take some time to consider the folded form. This can be organic, uneven folding or more uniform and measured, should you prefer a more ordered format.

1. Work the piece in your hands, manipulating the surface to find the natural folds and creases. Work the folds in with your fingers, pressing firmly along the creases.

2. Should you wish, you could stitch the folds in place to create a firm edge. In this example, I have left a folded edge which offers the option to change the folds and rearrange the form.

3. To finish the work, apply a coat of acrylic wax. This brings out the colour, seals the surface and stiffens the cloth. You may need to work the folds again once the acrylic wax has dried thoroughly.

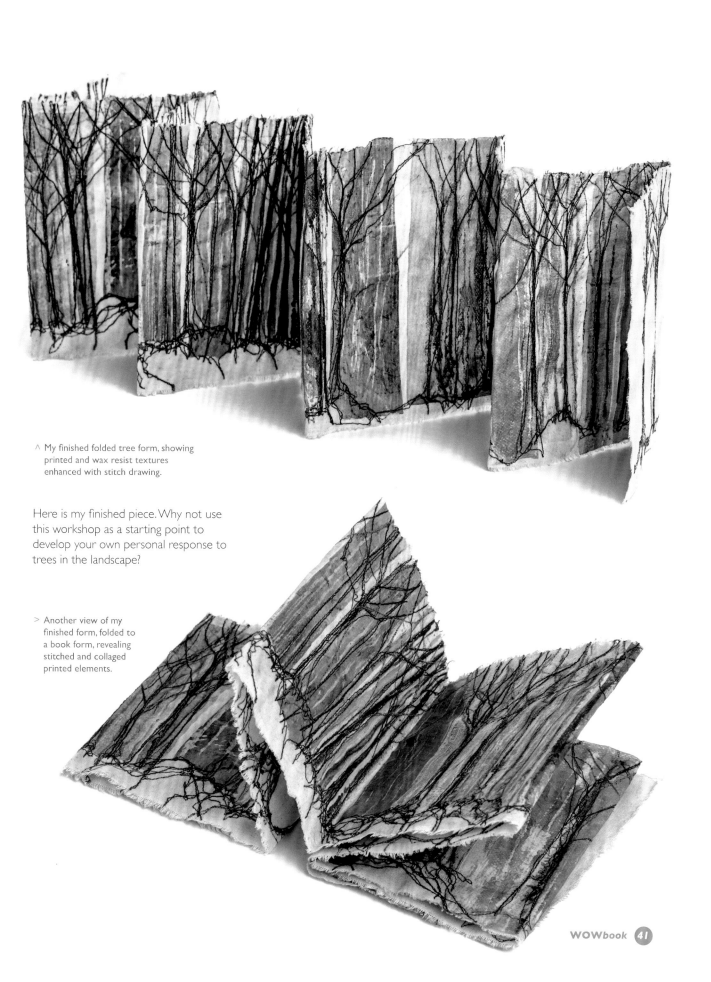

^ My finished folded tree form, showing
  printed and wax resist textures
  enhanced with stitch drawing.

Here is my finished piece. Why not use
this workshop as a starting point to
develop your own personal response to
trees in the landscape?

> Another view of my
  finished form, folded to
  a book form, revealing
  stitched and collaged
  printed elements.

Living by the sea in Cornwall, UK, I am constantly inspired by my surroundings and by peaceful times walking on the beach, enjoying the ever changing landscape, looking closely at nature, patterns, textures and tones of colour.

I am spoilt for choice for beaches to explore. Each one, I find, has its own particular specialty. You get to know where to look for beach pottery, seaweed, shells, etc. The beaches at St Ives inspire much of my work and I'm also in love with the tiny white-washed cottages with their lichen-yellow rooftops which sit around the harbour.

I enjoy the gathering process very much; exploring the shoreline, rock pools and beach streams, looking closely for the tiniest pieces of flotsam and jetsam.

I photograph these *in situ* along the beach and, inevitably, small beachcombing finds come home with me in the pockets of my dress. Intriguing mussel shells with barnacles, pebbles, limpets, tangles of seaweed, snippets of beach string, interesting pieces of beach-smoothed pottery, sea-washed glass and driftwood.

As well as taking many photos, I paint and make small drawings and notes. I also find myself reminiscing about childhood holidays, and all these things combined inspire me.

My beachcombing finds are carefully washed and then arranged and displayed as still-life vignettes which I photograph with nostalgic, vintage seaside photos and words. They further inspire memories, stories and imaginings in my head. They speak to me and I find I'm drawn to them, using the finds in my textile work, collages, paintings and photographs.

I like to work in a variety of media and materials. Texture and colour are most important to me. Experimenting with texture in different media is what I love, especially with layering, and I am drawn to tones of colour associated with my part of Cornwall. I also love to work seasonally, exploring nature in the hedgerows and landscapes, as well as on the beach and among seascapes. Nuances of each season influence my work.

As I start to work on a textile piece, layers of texture are built up with fabrics, paints, my beach finds and whatever else is to hand. I may start with one idea but as the pieces are laid out,

they tend to take on a story of their own. I go along with the way the pieces interact together. The gathering and selection process is what I love most: choosing which fabrics to use and where to place them. Often, my own hand-dyed fabrics are used and these are mixed with small pieces of vintage fabrics and lace. I indulge my interest in assemblage by using other unusual found objects from my collections as well as my beach finds. When I'm happy with the placement, these pieces are secured with creative, decorative, visible and invisible stitches. I love losing myself in every aspect of this creative process. At each stage, time for reflection is allowed and I find that while working on one piece, other ideas flood in. It is the most enjoyable thing!

Find out more about Carolyn and her work here: ***www.carolynsaxby.blogspot.com*** and website at ***www.carolynsaxby.co.uk***

> From left to right

Winter beachcombing. Inspired by a beautiful early morning of winter beachcombing, this heart has some very pretty details. The shells were found on the beach at Marazion and mixed with fine embroidery, lace, beads and tiny knots. At the bottom, I added some further beading with a small stack of buttons and a real limpet shell. Working on a background of softest silk, I have layered up silver snowflakes, fine frayed grey chiffon and scrim on top of the silk.

Snowed-in cottage on the beach. When it snows in Cornwall, it's a rare treat to see the beaches white and peaceful. This Cornish cottage sits right on the water's edge, where frothy surf meets whitest snow. I've used many layers of melted chiffon for the snow drifts that settle on the ridges of sand on the harbour beach. Lots of little white knots were stitched for texture on hand painted fabric.

When the mist rolled in from the sea. A darling baby heart stitched on white dupion silk with hand-dyed sea-coloured habotai silk. I used wispy, frothy, melted chiffon and book binding textures secured with tiny stitches and words from an old book. Fine Cornish mist can roll in from the sea and enigmatically change a scene and atmosphere in an instant. I simply added some little knots, beads, crystals and snowflakes.

the mist rolled in from the sea

INSPIRED BY...

BIRDS
with *Suzette Smart*

I am a textile artist living and working in a rural hamlet in north Shropshire, UK. The birds, animals and landscape outside my door, as well as along the towpath close by, are my greatest source of inspiration for stitching and storytelling. The conversion of our children's treehouse to a bird hide is the ideal place to observe, up close, the characters and beauty of the garden birds that visit our home. With a cup of coffee and a piece of cake, it's the perfect retreat.

By talking to others, you become aware that particular birds have significance for different people. It might be that they are seen as a forecaster, signifying good fortune (or maybe not), a reincarnation of a loved one or the promise of spring and good weather. Within a piece of my work, I attach meanings to certain birds as to what they have come to mean to me. They are an important part of the visual and hidden story being created. For example, the traits of the jay make him my current favourite narrator. He's quite a secretive bird but quietly observes the goings-on of the day. The blue tit is another favourite and always welcome in a piece of work for the joy that they bring. Their mischievous masks and sense of fun appear to me as happiness personified.

The initial inspiration for the piece of work, *Come to tea, said the great tit to me* was found in the inky elderberries that I brought into my studio. They looked so delicious that I couldn't resist drawing them in thread. As I worked, I quickly thought of them as food for the birds and sought to find a tea-time tale to tell. I took the drawing so far and then, using my own childhood dress as a pattern, cut a piece of embroidered fabric to fit the panels and made a collar. It was a little bit of a jigsaw to find the perfect piece but once discovered, I could reassemble by layering and patching where necessary. A great tit and a blue tit were then added and the piece was developed further with more fabric collage, free machine embroidery and a little hand stitch. The only thing left to include was a stitched invitation, which reads: 'Come to tea, said the great tit to me, and we shall dine on jam and wine.'

When selecting and sourcing materials for a bird and a piece of work, I prefer to use those which are having their second life. This includes upcycled sari silks, scarves, clothing and sometimes, other people's scraps! I love working with this

∧ *A song for my lovely far, far away.* My foundation fabric for this piece was a beautifully edged napkin. I have also used repurposed fabrics for the collage with free machine embroidery, hand stitch and a little mixed-media. The monogram from the napkin has been included too.

eclectic mix of plain and patterned fabrics where there is always a surprise. So just as there are layers within the story, the same can definitely be said for the fabric and thread. Once I'm happy that all these pieces are blended, a little bit of seed stitch often has the last say.

You can see more of Suzette's work on her website at *www.suzettesmart.com*

< Come to tea, said the great tit to me, and we shall dine on jam and wine. After sketching a branch of elderberries for this piece in thread, I added the colours and textures of the beech hedge that sits outside my studio window. This was then cut up to fit the dress pattern and developed further with the addition of a great tit, blue tit and an invitation to tea! For this piece, I used a variety of repurposed fabrics including sari silks, a napkin and a scarf which are held in place by free machine embroidery. The story was completed by hand with a little seed stitch.

INSPIRED BY...

BLANKETS, BILLETS AND BURNING

with *Janette Bright*

Back in 2003, when seeking inspiration for my textile work, I discovered the story of the London Foundling Hospital. Opened in 1741, the institution's aim was to rescue infants from death or poverty and turn them into 'useful citizens'. Parents bringing children to the hospital would leave an object, a note or a piece of textile such as a snippet of blanket. These identifiers (commonly known as tokens) were wrapped in an admission document known as a billet – not to be opened unless the 'foundling' was ever reclaimed. What was then an interesting discovery became a life-changing moment for me.

I began to research the hospital, the children and, where possible, the parents who left them. Telling their stories began to feed into my own creative work. As many of the tokens were fabrics and ribbon, and so much of the mothers' lives spent stitching and washing, textiles seemed the most appropriate medium for my work. Most of my work is three-dimensional and I like the idea of their stories being 'hidden' behind symbols; much like the foundling tokens, their histories never fully known.

Along the way, I have created infant clothing based on eighteenth-century examples, abstract figure pieces and many hearts. Hearts are frequently referenced in the billet books. One of the mothers I have returned to again and again is Margaret Larney, a woman executed by burning, who left two sons at the hospital in 1758. For each of her boys, I created an infant gown, tied with red tape to symbolise the documents in the archives. The gowns are embellished with sewing equipment (a pincushion and scissors) as records show that Margaret made her living through needlework. The flowers on the gowns include fabric printed with the account of Margaret's crime, and stitched hands to symbolise her 'handing' the children on.

Another piece came from a single line in the archive. A foundling girl had talked of a gift 'of trifling value', referring to its sentimental value. Its more important monetary worth led to her escaping her cruel master as he demanded it for himself. I made her a new 'gift', a beaded heart, to tell her story but also, to consider the idea of value and what it means today compared to back then.

These tokens have been important to me for other reasons. My interest in them and in the Foundling Museum, where many are housed, led to becoming first a museum volunteer, then an author. Now I am a part-time PhD history student and I still work occasionally at the Foundling Museum. I have been particularly lucky to have been involved in some of their historical exhibitions including 'Threads of Feeling, Fate, Hope and Charity' and most recently, 'Ladies of Quality and Distinction'. I have also rediscovered my love of teaching adults beading and craft skills, which seems appropriate considering textiles were so important to the lives I research.

By continuing to stitch as part of the group E.A.S.T. (East Anglian Stitch Textiles), I can pursue my research and continue to tell narratives inspired by the Foundling Hospital archives.

More about Janette and her work can be seen here: *www.artisticthreads.blogspot.com*

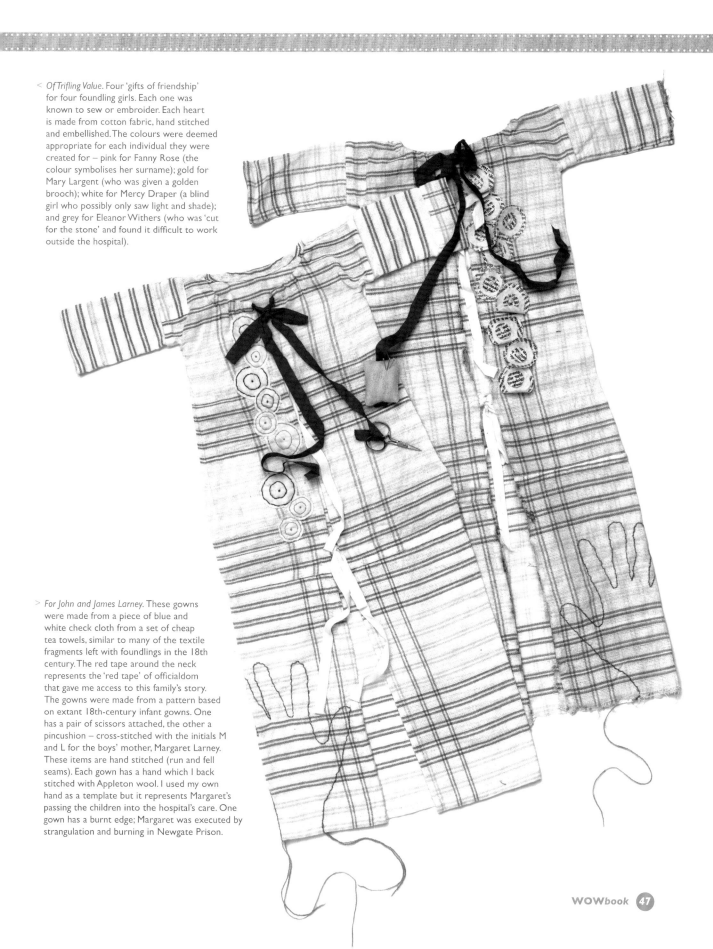

< *Of Trifling Value*. Four 'gifts of friendship' for four foundling girls. Each one was known to sew or embroider. Each heart is made from cotton fabric, hand stitched and embellished. The colours were deemed appropriate for each individual they were created for – pink for Fanny Rose (the colour symbolises her surname); gold for Mary Largent (who was given a golden brooch); white for Mercy Draper (a blind girl who possibly only saw light and shade); and grey for Eleanor Withers (who was 'cut for the stone' and found it difficult to work outside the hospital).

> *For John and James Larney*. These gowns were made from a piece of blue and white check cloth from a set of cheap tea towels, similar to many of the textile fragments left with foundlings in the 18th century. The red tape around the neck represents the 'red tape' of officialdom that gave me access to this family's story. The gowns were made from a pattern based on extant 18th-century infant gowns. One has a pair of scissors attached, the other a pincushion – cross-stitched with the initials M and L for the boys' mother, Margaret Larney. These items are hand stitched (run and fell seams). Each gown has a hand which I back stitched with Appleton wool. I used my own hand as a template but it represents Margaret's passing the children into the hospital's care. One gown has a burnt edge; Margaret was executed by strangulation and burning in Newgate Prison.

INSPIRED BY...

VENICE'S BLUE BALLS
with *Shirley Sherris*

Whenever my husband and I visit Venice, we like to go out in the late evening when there are few people about so we can take photographs unhindered.

Near to one of the waterbus landings is a sculpture: a huge metal spherical cage filled with blue plastic balls. At night, a light inside shines through the balls. This sculptural image became the design source for a number of textile pieces.

For my first piece, I designed a purse and tried to create a representation of the blue balls inside the cage. Many circles were cut from several shades of blue sheer fabric. A sandwich of lining, padding and background fabric represented the sheer blue balls, and a final layer of blue sheer fabric was machine stitched with a dark blue metallic thread replicating the metal cage.

Many other designs were created from the results of putting the source image into the computer and using several different design programs and filters. Any effects which rang design bells were saved and used to design more textile pieces. By adjusting some of the sliders in the program, different effects can be created. I chose three of them which were printed onto a cotton fabric using a flatfeed printer and pigment inks. Using pigment inks does not require treatment of the fabric as they do not bleed and are permanent. These prints were machine quilted and embellished with couched cords and beads. When complete, they were stretched and mounted.

My next idea was to create some hexagons by manipulating my original image with a design program on the computer, using a kaleidoscope filter before printing onto fabric. When printing the first of these hexagons, I realised I had not allowed

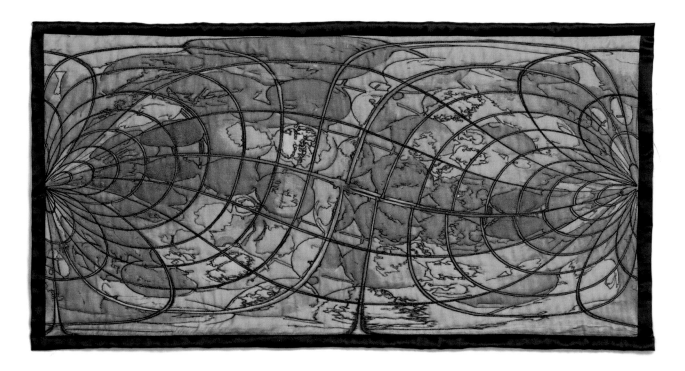

∧ A wall art quilt printed onto fabric using a distortion feature called *ornament*. The fabric has then been machine quilted and metallic paint used to highlight some of the features of the design.

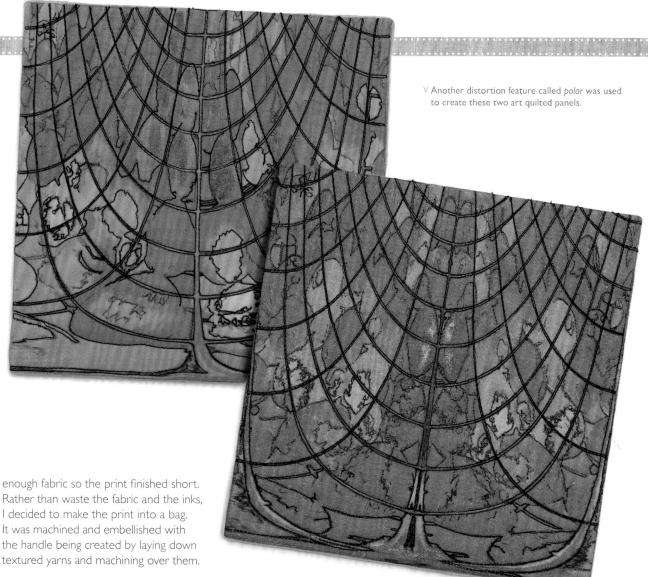

∨ Another distortion feature called *polar* was used to create these two art quilted panels.

enough fabric so the print finished short. Rather than waste the fabric and the inks, I decided to make the print into a bag. It was machined and embellished with the handle being created by laying down textured yarns and machining over them.

I then produced a piece that was the result of the distortion filter effect on the source image by computer program. This too was printed onto fabric and machine quilted onto dyed S80 Vilene to make the lining. The bottom 2 in (5 cm) was turned up to make the pockets of a keepsake folder.

Another design used a distortion filter called *ornament*. I enlarged and elongated the image and once again, printed it onto fabric. Fabrics absorb the ink and therefore reduce the vibrancy of the colours. To counteract this, I increased the saturation and vibrancy before printing. I machine quilted the piece and added some metallic paint to highlight some of the features of the design. It was then edged and became a wall art quilt.

A distortion filter called *polar* gave me another design. This was cut and pasted in order to provide two 8 x 8 in (20 x 20 cm) art quilted panels (above).

The final filter used was called *pattern*. I applied the filter creating patterns that I liked. Again, using the sliders gave different colour changes. I selected just one column from each of the patterns which were printed onto transfer paper then ironed onto dyed S80 Vilene. These were embellished with stitch, beads and embossing powders to make textile bookmarks and a bag-tag.

Using the computer is one way of creating original, unexpected and endless designs and colour schemes from one image, and there is scope to create many more pieces such as tassels and boxes. Have fun!

More information about Shirley and her work can be found at: *www.shirleyannesherris.blogspot.com*

INSPIRED BY...

BOWER HOUSES

with *Rachael Singleton*

This little piece all started with a question about what makes a room. Does a room need doors and/or windows?

I am inspired by nature and started to wonder about bowers as a type of room. I do marvel at bower birds and their crazy, bright collections – they are truly amazing! I also live in a small village called Hall Bower in West Yorkshire, England, and local inspiration from my walks led me to consider making a number of 'bower houses' celebrating the seasons: one definition of bower is 'a pleasant or shady place under trees'.

These little houses would be stylised, with no doors or windows as such, just a simple form to use as a shelter for treasure.

The bower house featured here is for the month of May. I have tried to capture the pale green of new leaves opening on the trees, producing the dappled light that shelters patches of bluebells.

I don't know about you but the arrival of bluebells in their purple-blue haze each year is always magical – and very elusive when trying to capture it on camera. Incidentally, many bower birds seem to prize blue objects highly.

Everything about this piece was experimental. The textile is a sandwich of dyed cotton, cotton batting and painted teabag paper, bonded to the wadding. It was lovely to stitch, being malleable and forgiving. I had produced a framework of salvaged, rusty metal mesh to build the bower house around but I ended up cutting all but the edges away, realising that I wanted to hide the mesh. What is left is just strong enough to maintain the shape. The leaves were stitched around in blanket stitch and filled with a thread pattern resembling the veins. I stitched across each gap in horizontal lines, from bottom to top, catching the thread fast at the top then looping it around each horizontal line, pulling down gently and tying it at the bottom.

The bluebells were also made by trial and error. I knew I wanted a less realistic representation and was trying out a number of options when – in a serendipitous moment – I found dowel could be pushed up through an art straw achieving a tight fit! A pair of wire cutters had small pieces of paper-covered dowel flying all over the studio but once retrieved, these small pieces were painted and wrapped in various threads. They were glued onto a separate base in small drifts.

The house has some small twigs attached. I do like a good twig and decided to include them to draw the eye more freely around the piece and to provide continuity with other bower houses I have made.

Having been so inspired by this subject, I leave you with a question to inspire your own thoughts: what kind of 'bowers' do you place your treasures in for safekeeping?

More of Rachael's work can be seen here:
www.folioandfibre.com

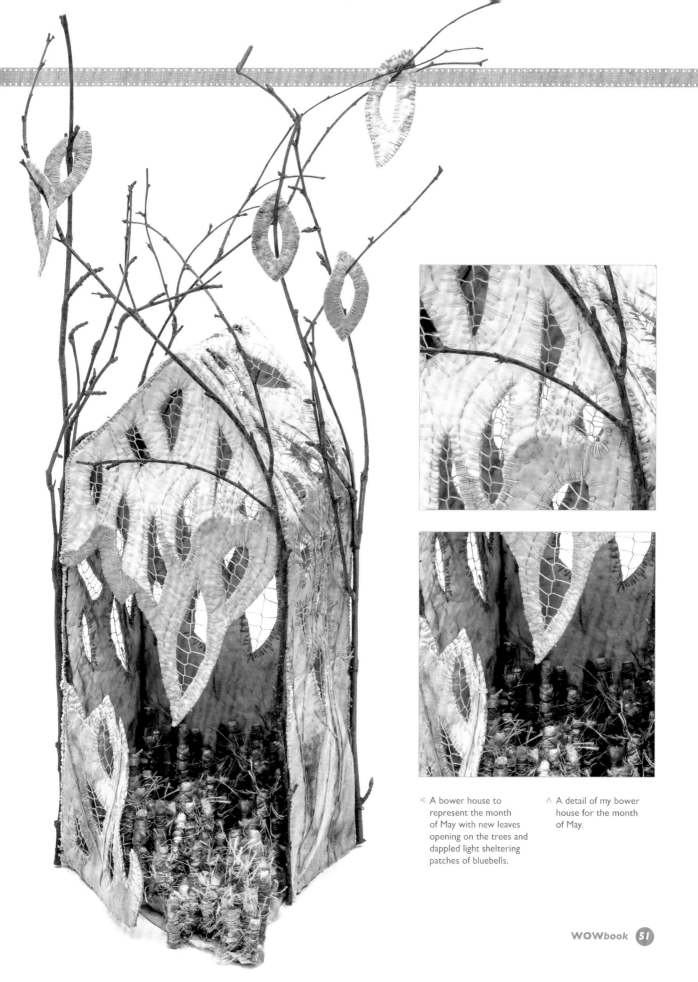

< A bower house to
represent the month
of May with new leaves
opening on the trees and
dappled light sheltering
patches of bluebells.

∧ A detail of my bower
house for the month
of May.

100 YEARS HABERDASHERY
Transforming a pre-loved sewing box

Anne Kelly

The idea for this project developed through the making of a heart for the '100 Hearts – War Stories' campaign by the Embroiderers' Guild.

I made two hearts, one for the touring exhibition and one for an exhibition in Canada at the Mississippi Valley Textile Museum, which is a lovely old mill turned museum in Ontario, near Ottawa. The hearts were based on some photographs that I found from my mother's family and her ancestors who were involved in the conflict of World War II.

Vintage sewing boxes and haberdashery are endlessly fascinating for the textile artist and we often collect them. The packaging, faded colours and thoughts of the hands that have passed across their surfaces evoke memories and ideas of the histories and stories that must have surrounded them. The flat surfaces of a sewing box or small wooden box provide a great framing device for these items. The folding shelves inside them create vitrines to display small selections of items. I found my first original sewing box at a jumble sale in Jersey, whilst teaching there, and thought it would be good to use a variety of family photos, haberdashery items, ephemera and stitched textiles to cover it.

I am a great believer in using 'best' from your stash and not saving it indefinitely. The sad fact is that no one will love it more than you or make something more meaningful with it. It is heartbreaking to see the cumulative hours of painstaking vintage textile work that ends up in charity shops or even discarded. To preserve old textiles they need to be kept at a stable temperature and will eventually decay if not. The joy of preserving and making something new with old treasures is wonderful and a great way of sharing your love for them. The same can be said for old paper, books and ephemera, which are also not considered of any value and can yet be ideal for projects. These items can be found quite easily in charity shops, markets and jumble sales.

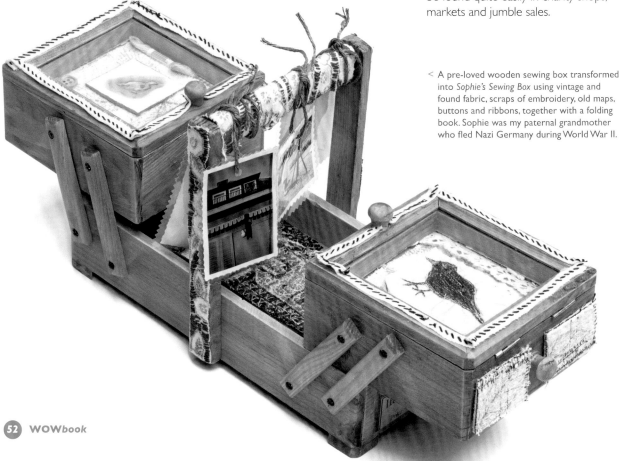

< A pre-loved wooden sewing box transformed into *Sophie's Sewing Box* using vintage and found fabric, scraps of embroidery, old maps, buttons and ribbons, together with a folding book. Sophie was my paternal grandmother who fled Nazi Germany during World War II.

Sophie's Sewing Box

For this project, I have created a sewing box in memory of my paternal grandmother, Sophie, who fled Nazi Germany in 1939 for London, and lived in north London until her death in 1979. She was a wonderful granny and loved her garden, so I have used a combination of references to her home in the UK and family photographs to create a new version of the haberdashery sewing box. I have also made a small folding book to fit inside the box as part of the theme.

YOU WILL NEED:

- A wooden box with relatively smooth surfaces
- Vintage papers – pages from old books, maps or vintage-style wrapping paper
- Fabric remnants and scraps of embroidery, buttons and ribbons
- PVA glue
- Acrylic wax or acrylic varnish
- Glue stick
- Glue gun or heavy-duty glue
- An old book with an interesting spine and cover that will fit inside the box
- Scrap paper for templates
- Copies of relevant photos and documents

FOR THE BOOK:

- Thin pieces of fabric or paper that fit with the theme, 4 × 13½ in (10 × 35 cm)
- Backing paper or fabric, 4 × 13½ in (10 × 35 cm)
- Organza or tissue paper

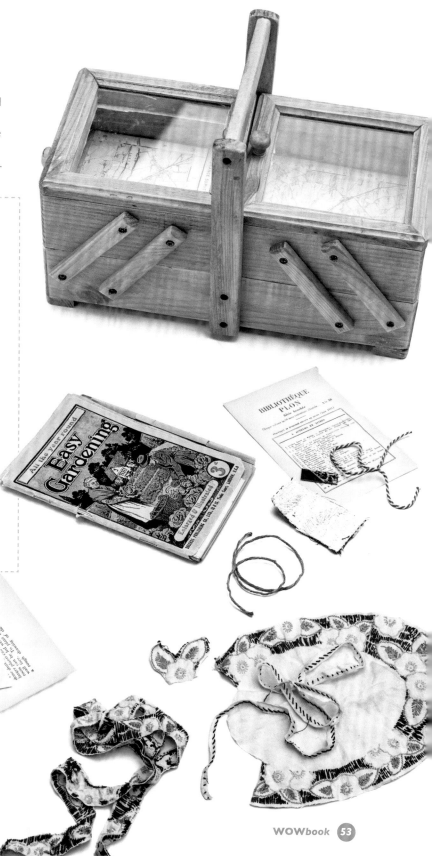

< An old map has been used to line the inside of the box. These can be picked up cheaply from car boot sales, markets or eBay. The one I used for this project is a vintage paper map of Hertford which has browned with age. You can achieve this look with a used teabag should you wish to age your map.

TIP
Make templates from scrap paper to use when cutting pieces to cover the surface of your box.

Lining the box

Cover any exposed and untreated surfaces on the inside of the box with a layer of paper. Here, an old map attached to a scrim backing has been used. Attach the papers securely to the scrim with a glue stick.

Samples

Select a few favourite pieces of embroidery, cross stitch or even samples from workshops and courses you have been on. Trim these so that they stand out and their backing cloth fades into the background. Place them around the box where they fit in. Use a glue gun or a heavy-duty glue to adhere them in position.

∨ Samples of embroidery trimmed to shape. These are some scraps of embroidery that I had on my work table, cut from a larger piece and which I thought would add to the decoration of the box. This is a good way to use up leftover pieces of work.

∧ Place the samples around the box and glue them to the surface. Place them around the box first to see where you feel they would fit in before glueing in place.

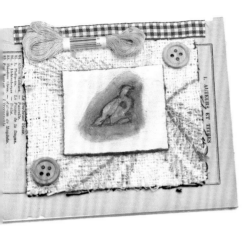

Collages made from small pieces of work and fragments. These little collages are made using older pieces of work – a painting of a bird and an embroidery. They have been embellished with lace and small haberdashery items including a few buttons and a skein of thread. The bases of the boards are covered in book pages and finally, all items have been glued onto the background.

Small collages

The top two trays of the sewing box have been used to make small collages with fragments from the studio and small pieces of work. These will be inserted when the rest of the work on the box is complete. The collage has been glued together with a small glue gun. I used part of the book's back cover as bases for the collages.

These small embroidered collages have been positioned in the top trays of the sewing box for maximum effect.

Vintage book

A vintage book with a beautifully decorated spine has been placed across the interior base of the sewing box. The spine has been removed and glued onto the cover so it could be viewed. Some pages have been removed from the book to make it fit better into the box.

I made a small folding book after finding a copy of my grandmother's exit document from Germany in 1939. I wanted to create a physical memory of her journey to go inside the box. I combined an old London map, copies of the document and textile remnants to make the book.

Remove pages from a vintage book, if necessary, to enable them to fit in the box. These can be trimmed to size and used to line your box.

Make a folding book

The book can be made in any size that will fit neatly into your box. Use a suitable base such as a medium-weight calico.

1. For the inside of the book, place your found papers and fabric remnants on the base fabric and secure them with the glue stick.

2. Cover with a layer of organza or tissue paper and coat with a diluted mixture of 50% PVA glue and 50% water. Allow to dry thoroughly.

3. For the cover of the book, use the same size paper or fabric as your base. I have used an old map of London. Once again, secure to the base fabric with glue stick, cover with organza or tissue paper and coat with the PVA mix.

4. When the book is thoroughly dry, machine stitch around the edges to neaten. You can stitch or embellish the cover and the inside pages further if you wish.

∧ This is the inside of the folding book showing found papers and fabric remnants. The piece was assembled according to the steps in this article and I added some thin pieces of fabric (torn cotton), fabric remnants and photocopied pages. When collating them, check first that the ink on your photocopy doesn't run.

∨ Here is the cover of my folding book. I have neatened the edges and hand stitched to add a bit of interest. You can embellish your book in any way you wish. The reverse side was made from a found map book of London. I used back stitch to finish the edges of my book.

Laminated photographs

I found some duplicated family photos which have been laminated for protection. The edges are trimmed with pinking shears to give them a vintage feel. They will be tied to the handle of the sewing box at the end of the making process.

< These family photographs have been laminated for protection. I have trimmed the edges with pinking shears to give them a vintage feel. Black and white photos are particularly good for this project as they already have an aged look. Old sepia photographs are even better!

< The handle of the box has been trimmed with embroidered pieces of fabric. I twisted some scraps of embroidered fabrics around the handle and glued them into place. My laminated photographs were then tied onto the handle with string threaded through holes punched into the photos' top edges.

TIP
Why not decorate your box with thread spools, needle packets and other vintage sewing ephemera?

Finishing

Now you are ready to finish decorating your box.

1. Place your collages or pieces of ephemera into the drawers you have allocated for them.

2. At this stage, you may also decide to decorate your box with pieces of ribbon or further embellishments like buttons or vintage haberdashery items. Use a glue gun to attach them securely to the box.

3. Use trim from embroidery pieces to cover the handle of the box, top and sides.

Varnishing the box

When you are happy with the look and position of the items and objects in your box, you are ready to varnish the piece. Use an acrylic varnish or acrylic wax with a stiff brush. Depending on the texture and the thickness of the items you have glued into and on the outside of the box, you may need two or more coats. Allow to dry completely before re-coating.

I am really pleased with *Sophie's Sewing Box*. It brings back many memories of my wonderful grandmother every time I look at it. I do hope you will create a box that will elicit similar memories for you.

< Apply two or more coats of acrylic wax or varnish to the box with a stiff brush.

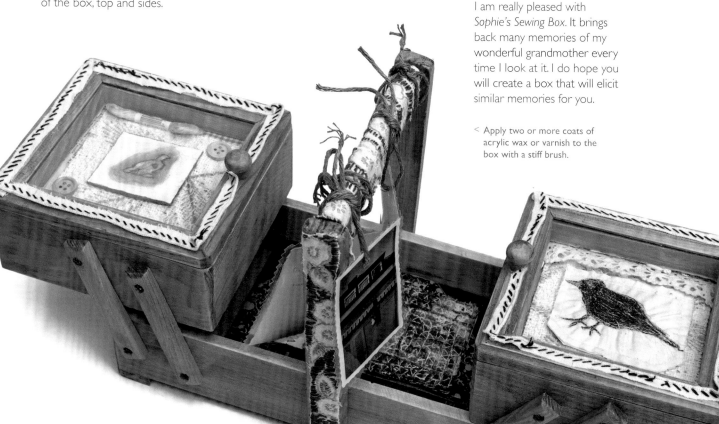

QUILTING ART
Lynda Monk talks to Sandra Meech

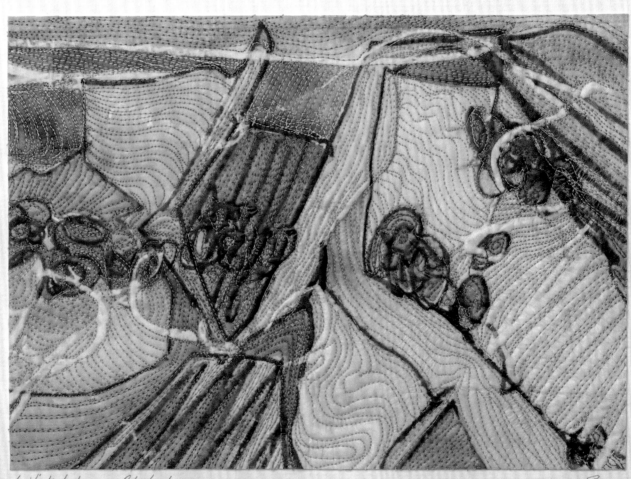

White Lake in Glastonbury

∧ *White Lake near Glastonbury.* Many of these more colourful pieces reflect the seasonal changes in colour and agricultural marks. This piece was inspired by the hills nearby and the Cary River with autumn harvest colours. They form part of a series *Marking Time*. Many of the shapes in these more abstract pieces are in response to aerial views seen on Google Earth, and the patchwork of natural and man-made marks on the landscape. *White Lake* began as an A4 mono print in black. I then took copies of it and, using wax resist to produce energetic lines, added a wash of bright watercolour to the surface. A jpg image of the watercolour was printed and transferred onto cloth with machine stitch. I enjoy the free machine drawing with thread for the detail.

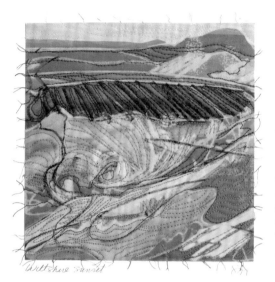

< *Wiltshire Sunset* and *Bratton Hilll*. These are the hills of Salisbury Plain in Wiltshire, UK. Driving frequently on the A303, you see huge vistas, big skies and the marks on the fields all through the year. These are very colourful, small pieces, and I wanted the abstract quality to be more pronounced. They began as mono prints onto heat transfer paper, which were ironed onto cloth with stitch added. They have also been painted (with resist lines added first) with a bright watercolour.

Q I understand that you studied at the Ontario College of Art in Toronto, Canada, Sandra. Who or what inspired and influenced you to start creating contemporary quilts?

A The Ontario College of Art, in those days, offered a fine art degree with a variety of painting and disciplines – life drawing, museum studies and the history of art. In the last two years, we specialised in either the commercial side of advertising, interior design and industrial design, or fine art – painting, sculpture or the applied art of textiles (weaving). I decided on the commercial side and the course on advertising and graphic design included illustration, typography and mixed-media. I hoped this would give me the better chance of finding a job. Working in the art department for a major publishing house, Maclean Hunter, enabled me to continue doing illustration, layout and design for advertisements and brochures, and later I worked there as an art director. These were the days before computers and clipart, so I continued with 'hands on' drawing and illustration using coloured pencils and gouache, whatever the subject matter.

The company brought me to their London office in 1975 and I stayed permanently in the UK, continuing to freelance in advertising and brochure design until 2004.

Living near Windsor, England, in the mid 1990s, I visited the graduate show at East Berkshire College and was overwhelmed by the contemporary quilts and textiles I saw there. They were abstract and expressive and appealed to the graphic designer in me. I learned machine sewing skills at an early age from a family of machine stitchers, so the City & Guilds course in contemporary quilting appealed to me.

Due to my art background, I was able to apply for a diploma in stitched textiles with Jan Beaney and Jean Littlejohn, and my work moved away from piecing, enabling me to explore different approaches that included hand stitch.

So, with a mixture of these early skills and the qualification for teaching in adult education, I embarked on a further fifteen-year freelance teaching career, concentrating on surface design, imagery, composition and stitch.

Q Do you have a favoured stitch, technique or fabric that you prefer to work with?

A I have always loved photography (particularly black and white photography at college) so using transferred imagery on cloth became a popular technique for me. At first, coloured and black and white photos were combined with painted, dyed and commercial fabrics. More recently, drawings, mono prints, paintings and collaged sketchbook pages have been my starting points.

Originally, I used 'Picture This', an acrylic medium spread thinly over laserjet printed photos. A copy is then laid, face down, onto thin white cotton. This is air dried, soaked with water and the paper side of the original copy is rubbed off to reveal the image. It's quite a long-winded process but very effective.

In the last ten years, I have been using heat transfer inkjet papers that are ironed, face down, onto cotton for similar results. Imagery on cloth over the years has become my 'signature' technique. I can create and manage this imagery in my own studio without the need for digital print services. Appreciating that today's textile design students need to understand and use the latest industrial print methods for their own work experience, my joy is being in total control and working through the various stages on my own.

∨ *Across Keysley Down.* A mono print in black. This was copied and then painted, photographed, heat transferred and stitched. This piece illustrates another season, the rolling hills and dark skies. My work continues to become more colourful – a contrast to the more muted palette that I used before in my work. I embraced this colourful challenge and surprised myself, really enjoying interpreting my local landscape with this kind of exuberance and looking at the colours through the seasons.

Across Keysley Down

sm.

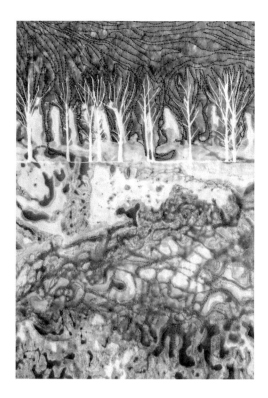
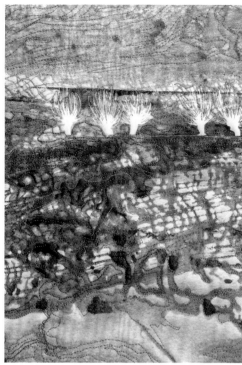

< *Winter Flood 1* and *Winter Flood 2.*
During our first two winters living in Somerton, Somerset, we experienced the flooding on the Somerset Levels. A natural occurrence, the winter of 2014 brought a particular combination of events: very high tides and a great deal of rain which swelled the main rivers that come inland from the sea as far as Yeovil and beyond. Fortunately, we live on higher ground but many villages and farms became isolated.

Q You have written four amazing books so far: *Creative Quilts, Contemporary Quilts, Connecting Art to Stitch* and *Connecting Design to Stitch*. These are so inspirational! If you had to choose a favourite, which one would it be and why?

A My first two books explored the working design methods and surface embellishment that I was teaching at the time. Frequently asked about the challenging next step after a good techniques-driven course, I suggested that a foundation art course might be a good idea. The student could gain more confidence with methods, composition and design. *Connecting Art to Stitch* was created to encourage the connection between basic art practice and how we might use these materials in contemporary textiles. This is my favourite book. It was like coming home for me – back to the essential basics of art and in my current work, what I wanted to say as a stitched textile artist. I followed this with a sister publication *Connecting Design to Stitch* which addressed the important contribution of the principles and elements of design in textile work.

Q Your books *Connecting Art to Stitch* and *Connecting Design to Stitch* deal with the stumbling blocks that many of us face. Although the books go into great detail, can you tell us briefly here how we may overcome this?

A Practise, practise, practise, always 'looking' and 'seeing'. Reading about art and design and learning the skills to illustrate this are the first steps. However, being consistently successful every time is not a quick fix.

I think, rather than become seduced by materials and techniques, we should focus on the whole composition of the piece. Any work that is wall-hung should be seen in the same way as we view art. It should work from a distance, then intrigue the viewer to step closer so they can see the materials used and the way stitch enhances the detail on closer inspection. If the composition or use of colour does not work, viewers will walk right by.

Design and composition are important to me. I constantly look at paintings – how the artist has directed our eye to a focal point, used light and shade or directional elements to keep constant interest across the surface. Even magazine spreads (the quality publications about interiors, travel, etc.) will use the same strategy in their placement of words, images and photos, leading one into the spread and around to the important features.

I often suggest using the line and shape in a painting as a starting point for our own collaged material – borrowing from the masters, perhaps.

Q Can you explain why sketchbooks are such an important part of your creative process?

A Sketchbooks are my starting point for most themes I have developed over the years. I create some pages *in situ* and others, using photographs or written observation. I love the process and could work into a sketchbook for quite some time as I develop ideas for future work. My sketchbook pages include drawing, painting, coloured pencil work and collage, with black and white photocopies sometimes using extended line, marks, writings and tracings. This process consolidates ideas, in a confined space. These sketch/collage pages are photographed or scanned and larger work developed. Working this way is an exciting, energetic yet calming experience for me, rather than designing on a planning wall. I have been using the long Seawhite accordion books recently and find the double-sided quality paper wonderful to work on. I also create small bound journal/sketchbooks for personal use (they are small,

chunky and square) and I usually make one for themes I might like to explore further.

I first start a new sketchbook with a photo reference nearby, and on the white pages, create some blind drawings with a wax resist. This creates an energetic line before I start painting the whole book at the same time with either Brusho or a strong watercolour. Dilute acrylic inks work too. Then I use coloured pencils, pens and markers to bring more detail into the pages. Choosing the pages for future work can vary in size from one to four (or more) spreads. If more than one page is used, I photograph the opened pages together and use Photoshop Elements and the clone stamp to blend the images together, dispensing with the fold mark. This way, I have a potential painting for printing and transferring onto cloth. I take sketchbooks everywhere and continue to make them for new themes in my work or as an *aide memoire* for a holiday or experience I want to record.

reflected image – grasses in water

∧ My sketchbooks. Here I have torn pages with different black and white and painted papers, adding marks with coloured pencils and pen. Some images are pasted into the book and I use collage on many pages. Tracing paper is added in every signature and it allows for tracing and mark making as well as a faded image underneath. These sketchbooks are a personal exploration and any ideas for stitching and finishing could be added on the pages.

< Pages of my sketchbooks are often torn to create a contrasting view which could suggest a way forward for a new piece of work. Here, a page with tracing paper over a black and white copy is used for mark making. This could suggest work on sheers or inspiration for stitch lines. Whenever lines are made on tracing paper, the whole image is not drawn but often becomes a suggestion of the shapes underneath as some of the detail is eliminated.

Q You refer to a 'sense of place' as one of the most alluring subjects to draw, paint or stitch. Where is or where would be your ideal sense of place?

A As a transplanted Canadian living in the UK for over forty years, being comfortable in my environment is very important. I love the countryside and am inspired by wide open spaces, big skies, the seasons and man-made and natural marks in the landscape, rather than city life. However, I do like architecture, pattern in buildings, industrial imagery and evidence of rust and decay. I take photos wherever I am.

We moved from East Berkshire to the quiet and beautiful hills of Somerset six years ago and it has become home for me. We are not far from the Somerset Levels and experienced two winters of flooded fields not far away, a phenomenon that has occurred for centuries. It inspired me to develop a series based on the history and environmental impact of flooding of the Levels.

This has become my ideal place: fresh air, big skies (they don't have to always be blue), experiencing the drama of the seasons, colour/weather/changes in the landscape and a connection to other textile friends and artists. Somerset has all this for me.

A large body of work called *Level Flood* has been made including my research into the history of the management of the Levels, combining this with the government's environmental response to it all. *Winter Flood 1* and *Winter Flood 2* began as collagraph prints in the muted muddy colours you see. The prints were photographed and the computer used to add a negative line image of the pollarded willow and birch trees in each piece. This gave a horizon line and brought the reality of the subject to the surface. The whole image was printed onto heat transfer papers and ironed onto white cloth layered, as I do with all my pieces, with S80 Vilene, and machine stitched. With all of this series of work, whatever the colour or interpretation of the landscape, I wanted the viewer to see it as an artistic interpretation first, then come closer to see the stitch.

∧ *Level Flood* sketchbook spread. This has a colour copy of the landscape with black marks on tracing paper pasted on top. The transparent quality indicates sheers, perhaps, or hand or machine stitch lines added to the surface. Most of the time, these pages just suggest ideas for future work. I could work into sketchbooks for weeks before starting an actual piece.

∨ *Level Flood* series sketchbook. Moving to the West Country, UK in 2012 from Berkshire was instrumental in a change of focus for me. I wanted to get back to some painting and life drawing while continuing to exhibit in stitched textile groups in the UK and Europe. My own created bound books have an interesting mix of printed surfaces. Working to a specific theme, I use colour copies, black and white copies (some painted with Brusho), and pages of writing and tracing paper.

Q I understand you have some new work in progress. Can you share some of it with us and your thought processes behind it?

A After moving to Somerton, I decided to spend more time getting back to art – back to my roots – by taking life drawing and the occasional painting class. My art and textile work based on Somerset was first inspired by the flooding and it included photographic images, collaged material and writings about the historical and environmental aspects of the area. As the fields recovered, more colour was revealed and my recent work has been based entirely on paintings, sketches and mono prints. In paintings, resists are used – lines to capture the energy I see in the landscape. These are usually from photographs or sketches and the memory of a place. Laying watercolour dye paints on top with an abstracted landscape in mind, pages are filled with colour quickly. Once dry, I then add more detail from observations, map marks or photos. Sections of these sketch paintings are photographed, printed and transferred onto cloth to inspire the new work. One of the major changes recently is the amount of machine stitching done on each piece. I have always enjoyed drawing with stitch and am taking full advantage of this at the moment.

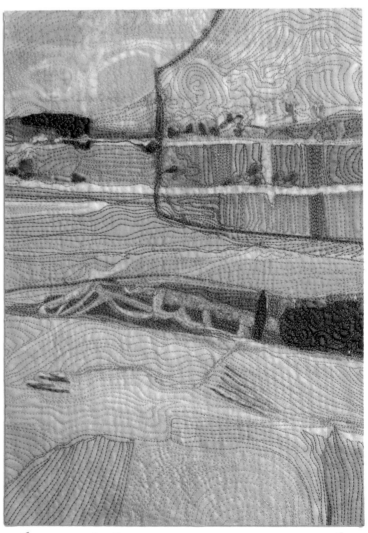

Coast II. The Falklands   *SM*

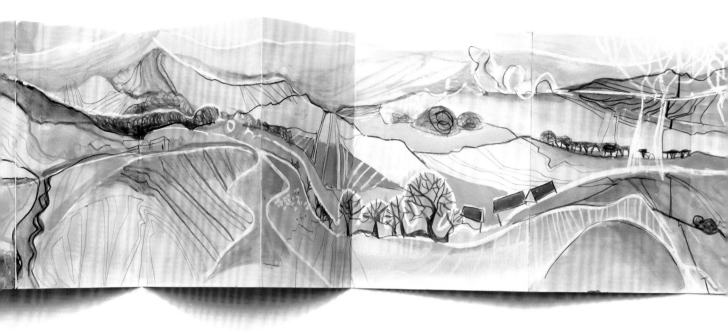

< *Coast II The Falklands.* By 2016, there were two groups I exhibited with and, timed with a trip to Antarctica and the Falklands (ice and glaciers being my constant passion), I created this piece. With sketchbook in hand, a few small watercolour sketches inspired this work. Not exactly Somerset, but I was struck by the rolling, bare hills and colours of the tundra outside Stanley. A photograph of my sketchbook page was enlarged and transferred onto cloth with stitch added.

∧ *Marking Time* sketchbook. When the flooding subsided, months after that winter, the land returned to the colours I had grown to love. Planting began again and the agricultural marks in the landscape inspired more colourful art and stitch. I like the accordion-fold Seawhite-style sketchbook as a starting point for a new series of work, as it can be painted on both sides. This lighter side shows the pages that inspired many pieces in the *Marking Time* series. All the drawings on these pages were made *in situ* or from photos taken on drives through Somerset and Wiltshire – reflecting the large skies, colour changes through the seasons and the agricultural crop marks on the fields throughout the year.

∧ *Marking Time 1, 2* and *3.* These pieces, part of a group of nine square stitch paintings, were included in Studio 21's 'Colour Notes' exhibition at the Knitting and Stitching Shows in 2018. They formed part of my accordion sketchbook pages. I found sections that I particularly liked in the book and photographed them. More had to be done on the computer to remove the creased fold of the page and when I had the image, it was then printed onto heat transfer pages, ironed onto cotton and heavily stitched. These are worked on A3 size papers and carefully aligned when ironing to produce the square. The machine threads I am using now, Presencia, are from Spain and the range of colours is wonderful. Each of these pieces was based on the hills and vistas seen from the A303, and I will continue to add to the collection.

Sue Brown

I am an artist who uses printmaking to tell stories and I am inspired by process as much as by nature. My work springs from the pages of my sketchbooks and I develop carefully researched themes using the printmaking processes, particularly collagraph and gum arabic transfer printmaking.

I use my work to explore the relationships we have with our feathered garden visitors; I am fascinated by all things ornithological. From the smallest garden bird to characterful corvids, I describe them through card, glue and ink. My collagraphs are humorous and full of expression.

I have been making prints for many years; I find the technique completely absorbing but the inspiration of birds is the catalyst for my creativity. My father spent a great deal of time naming the birds that visited our garden, and wildlife programmes were the viewing of choice in our household. My father kept and bred budgerigars and finches, so there were birds inside and outside our home throughout my childhood.

All my images are developed from the personal encounters I have with birds: those that visit my garden and visits to Slimbridge, Birdland in Bourton-on-the-Water, and country walks.

Several years ago, I was fortunate enough to visit the man who breeds ravens for the Tower of London. He lived just outside Bristol and introduced me to Marley, a semi-tame raven with bags of character. Images of these intelligent birds have led to the repeated use of crows, jackdaws and magpies as motifs in my prints.

Printmaking has always been my working process. I am passionate about promoting the understanding of the artist print and the contemporary use of traditional craft techniques. I lead workshops and demonstrations for groups nationally in a wide variety of printmaking and mixed-media sketchbook processes.

Website: **www.theyardartspace.com**

> *Birds on the Line*. Hand and machine stitched textile collage with gum arabic transferred prints.

∨ *Magpie*. Vintage fabrics with hand and machine stitched textile collage and gum arabic transferred print.

Handmade by
Sue Brown

Wendy Dolan

I have always loved creating, and textiles provide a very versatile medium for my artwork. I have combined art and textiles since my teens, learning traditional embroidery techniques and combining them with painting and drawing.

On deciding that my career was to be in teaching, I looked for a course which would further my love of textiles. This took me to Brighton, UK, where I completed a four-year degree in art and textiles. The course introduced me to freehand machine embroidery and a variety of textile techniques, and I had an exciting time experimenting. After a few

years teaching in the primary sector, I studied for a diploma in creative embroidery and began exhibiting and selling my work. I moved into adult education while raising my young family, and have continued to share my skills with adults on courses and workshops, both at home and abroad.

The landscape, natural forms and architecture have been my main sources of inspiration over the years, and I have always tried to combine my love of line, form and texture. Working with natural fabrics, I choose them for their different textural qualities. Calico, cotton, scrim, muslin, linen, silk noil, cotton batting, crepe bandage, lace and broderie anglaise all have unique qualities and can be layered and stitched to create exciting backgrounds. Xpandaprint and horticultural fleece can add extra surface texture. Colour is added to the design using fabric paint and, having created a textured, painted background, I then work into the design with hand and machine surface stitching.

In my series *A Sense of Place*, I incorporate my love of maps into my work, using a method of transfer printing onto fabric. Architectural or landscape features are incorporated to make the designs very individual. I have worked on some exciting commissioned projects over the years, for both private and corporate clients, including large banners, wall-hangings and wedding dress embellishments. For my daughter's wedding dress, I made embroidered lace on fine tulle netting with freehand machine stitching.

Larger scale commissions create their own challenges and I have made two stage curtains for the Royal Caribbean cruise liners, 'Legend of the Seas' and 'Grandeur of the Seas'. *Starlight Serenade* and *Let's Dance* both measure 13.5 x 4.5 metres. With a colleague, Jae Maries, I designed and created a large Millennium wall-hung textile for Ashridge House in Hertfordshire, UK. Inspired by the history and surroundings of Ashridge, the design is a montage of images surrounded by a decorative border of motifs which were worked by members of staff, with our tuition and guidance.

Having exhibited my work for many years and shared my techniques and ideas with students, I wrote *Layer, Paint and Stitch* for Search Press in 2015. My book encourages experimenting with a variety of techniques and developing an individual style of work.

I am a Fellow of the Society of Designer Craftsmen and a member of the Sussex Guild, and regularly exhibit my artwork and demonstrate my techniques at exhibitions and shows.

Website: **www.wendydolan.co.uk**

Mapping the Downs. Inspired by a row of trees which I drive past on my way home over the Downs. This design incorporates layered and textured fabrics with a transfer printed map, machine and hand stitching.

Rugged Moors. Inspired by the rugged landscape of the Yorkshire Moors, with its windswept trees and rough jagged rocks. An assortment of fabrics are combined to create a rich surface and Xpandaprint adds to the crusty textures. Freehand machine stitching adds to the detail and definition of the design.

Anne Hellyer

I have enjoyed drawing and painting for as long as I can remember and at the age of six, my grandmother introduced me to her treadle sewing machine. I have been making things ever since.

As a child, I was never allowed to buy a kit but had to create things from scratch with whatever was available. I still love improvising and designing. I made my own clothes and once I had a family, made clothes for my children, but I kept my interest in art and in using textiles very separate.

In 1998, I joined the newly formed branch of the Embroiderers' Guild in Andover, Hampshire, UK. Here, I met Margaret Beal and realised there was more to embroidery than I first thought. In 2005, I was able to study for my City & Guilds in creative embroidery. At this point, a whole new textile world opened up before me. My tutor, Terrie Hitchcock, was very inspiring and encouraged me to incorporate my interest in art with my textile work. I loved every minute of the four year part-time course.

∧ *I Love Beer*. Beer is a seaside town in Devon, UK. The background was created with my hand-painted fabric and I added details with print and free machine embroidery. The piece is reinforced with wire mesh and block mounted to hang proud of the wall.

Once I had finished the course, I was full of new skills and ideas, and wanted to create my own style of work. I have always loved architecture and wanted the embroidery and texture of the fabrics to be 'unfettered' by glass or frame. After much experimenting, my free-standing textile art pieces were born.

The group of us who studied for City & Guilds together decided to continue working as a group. Ten years later, we are still meeting and exhibiting as 'Zero Nine Textile Artists'. Our website is at: *www.zeroninetextileartists.wordpress.com*

Website: *www.paintingthetown.org.uk*

ᐯ *London Skyline.* This piece was created with layers of my hand-painted fabric. Further details were added with print and free machine embroidery. It is reinforced with wire mesh and block mounted to hang and can also be shaped to be free-standing.

Amanda Hislop

My passion for colour and texture originated from my Art Foundation course at Newcastle College of Art and Design in the UK. This led to a degree in woven textiles with painting, which I studied at West Surrey College of Art and Design from 1983 to 1986. Drawing, sketching and painting are skills which are second nature to me, with art a key part of life. This is reflected in my love of sketchbooks, painting, drawing, threads and stitch.

Following my degree, I studied for a postgraduate teaching qualification in visual arts and then took a position as an art and textiles teacher in the independent sector. I moved to Wantage in Oxfordshire, UK, to teach A Level and GCSE art textiles at St Mary's, a small girls' boarding school. In my teaching, spanning nearly 20 years, I covered a wide range of textile processes including screen and block printing, felt making and machine stitching which I established as a key part of the art textiles department.

This wide experience in art and textiles instilled the knowledge, confidence and desire to follow a different course and in 2007, I took redundancy to follow a personal creative pathway as a textile artist and tutor.

∧ *Land Unfolds* – 35 x 18 x 1 in (89 x 45 x 2.5 cm). Lines suggest movement in landscapes. Working in line and the muted tones of an earthy colour palette, I combined layered papers, threads and stitch to reveal an unfolding landscape.

I teach widely throughout the UK with visits to Northern Ireland in 2014 and the Harbour Gallery in Jersey in 2017. I use my teaching skills and passion for sketchbooks, drawing, painting and stitch to deliver inspirational workshops to guilds and groups exploring textile processes and channelling the personal creative energy of individuals. In addition, I am an established tutor at Oxford Summer School, Art Van Go, Ardington School of Crafts and The Granary Studio, where I am able to offer a variety of workshops reflecting my working practice in fabric, paint and stitch. I also teach in the Art Studio at White Horse Bookshop in Marlborough, Wiltshire.

I have produced two self-published books: *Land lines: drawn lines: stitch lines* and *Reflections on trees, a sketchbook exploration* which I sell at shows and workshops. In 2016, I was thrilled to be commissioned to write a book for Search Press, *Stitched textiles: Seascapes*, which is to be

published in 2019. I have enjoyed the whole process that writing a book requires, from the analysis of my working practice to the selection of pieces and the creation of new work and samples. Needless to say, I took great pleasure in planning trips to the sea, taking my sketchbook and drawing materials, to record inspiration for the publication.

I am a member of both the Prism Textile Group and the Oxfordshire Craft Guild and exhibit regularly with both groups.

Website: *www.amandahisloptextileartist.com*

> *Cow parsley soft misty morning* – 19½ x 59 in (50 x 150 cm). An evocative piece inspired by the statuesque forms of the plant on a frosty, misty morning. I used layered papers, threads and paint on a cloth background.

∨ *Into the woods, lines and winter light* – 47¼ x 22½ x 2½ in (120 x 57 x 5 cm). Trees, reaching skyward, vertical lines, in a landscape largely defined by undulating horizontals. The warm light of winter dusk emphasises the linear qualities – captured in painted and stitched lines, echoing memories of trees. I used various densities of cotton fabrics with paper, paint and stitch.

Anne Kelly

I was born and educated in Canada and came to the UK on an art scholarship. After further study at Goldsmiths' College in London, I settled in the UK. I now live and work in my garden studio in Kent, UK.

My heavily embroidered fabric collages are reminiscent of tapestry work and my signature stitching technique is applied to a variety of surfaces, using mixed-media and print techniques, to further embellish my work. I am an award-winning textile artist, author and tutor, exhibiting and teaching nationally and internationally. My work is represented in private and public collections both in the UK and abroad.

I have initiated collaborations and fund-raising efforts with conservation and homelessness charities including the RSPB, Buglife and Shelter. Two of my curated community collaborations and exhibitions were featured in guest artist galleries at the Knitting and Stitching Shows at Alexandra Palace, Olympia, London, and in Dublin and Harrogate in 2016 and 2018. I have also participated in Embroiderers' Guild exhibitions and other group touring exhibitions.

I use reclaimed and recycled textiles to create new work. I like the feel and quality of these pieces, which are gifted or found, and believe in using simple, readily available materials.

Recently, I have covered objects and garments with my work – to popular acclaim. I was an invited artist to the Prague Patchwork Meeting and Quilt en Beaujolais, and was selected for the past three 'World of Threads' exhibitions in Canada. In 2019, I have two major exhibitions of work in Canada and Australia.

I am a busy tutor, often combining exhibition and teaching commitments. In 2019, I was an invited tutor for the second time to Timeless Textiles and two quilt retreats in Australia, as well as Fibre Arts New Zealand. I have worked with craft collections and institutions in the UK including the National Needlework Archive and the Ruthin Craft Centre in Wales. I was artist in residence at the Sussex Prairie Garden in 2014 and to the FIAF Farindola residency in Abruzzo in 2018.

My first book was *Connected Cloth*, co-written with Cas Holmes, and my second book, a solo project, *Textile Nature*, was published in 2016 by Batsford. My third publication *Textile Folk Art* came out in 2018 and links my continued interests in working with groups, nature conservation and folk art. I am currently working on a new book project and writing articles for blogs and textile magazines, nationally and internationally.

Website: **www.annekellytextiles.com**

> *Home Fires Dress*, 2018, Textile collage, 33½ x 35½ in (85 x 90 cm). This piece forms part of a series of 'dress' collages made for various exhibitions in 2018 and 2019. It was first shown at the Compton Verney Textile Fair, Warwickshire, UK, in November 2018 and formed part of my exhibition 'Articles of Ancestry' shown in Newcastle, Australia in April 2019. I like to use garments as a structural device in my work and am attracted to vintage dresses and embroidery. I have used a piece of a cross-stitched fireplace as well as a charity shop found dress. These were placed on top of an antique French textile found in a brocante shop near Limoges, France. The piece has been partially covered with translucent organza and overstitched with my signature Bernina edging stitch. Hand stitching has also been added.